BY KENNETH PHILLIPS

Signed, the President

Neighborhood Story Project

P.O. Box 19742

New Orleans, LA 70179

www.neighborhoodstoryproject.org

Editor: Rachel Breunlin

Publisher: Abram Himelstein

Graphic Designer: Gareth Breunlin

The printing of this book made possible by
a generous grant from the Lupin Foundation.

THE
LUPIN
FOUNDATION

ISBN-13: 978-1-60801-015-8

Library of Congress Control Number: 2009940212

http://unopress.uno.edu

Dedication

I dedicate this book to my family. Thank you for all the encouragement.

Acknowledgements

Thank you to my mom. I love you.

Thank you to my brothers Terrance and Kimani for always keeping me laughing.

Thank you to all my fellow classmates and teachers at the Neighborhood Story Project: Rachel and Abram, Lindsey and Lea, Money, Doo, Susan and Kareem—for all the help and support.

Thank you to my six interviewees: Mom, Terrance, Kimani, Grandma Loretta, Grandma Irma, and Loren. Y'all made this book come together.

Thank you to Ms. Marshall for the love and support and for keeping me in your prayers.

Thank you to Tweet for being a good friend and for making me go to class.

Thank you to Arie, Izzy, and Amber for standing by my side every step of the way.

Thank you to my cousins, Miesha, Misheka and Sameka, for teaching me how to stay and feel calm.

Thank you to the faculty and staff at John McDonogh for the encouragement. Ms. Pratt, Ms. Alaxander, Ms. Cooper, Brother Rob, and my "favorite teacher," Mrs. Jacob.

Thank you to my dawg "Wee-Wee"—always and forever my blood brother.

Thank you to Daphnie—you're a cool person. Stay cool and krazi.

Thank you to my grandmothers Loretta Martin and Irma Phillips for all the love and wisdom.

Thank you to Kobey, Grandpa Alfred, Messy Man, and Uncle Irvin—Gone But Never Forgotten. I love y'all to death.

Thank you to my daddy and his family. I look forward to seeing y'all soon.

Thank you to my sista Janeka Booker "Ne Damon."

Thank you to my book committee: Grandma Irma, Helen, and Johanna, for reading my book and helping it grow.

Thank you to Keith, Willie, Le Shelle and all my friends. Y'all keep me sane.

Table of Contents

Kenneth outside the St. Bernard, courtesy of the Neighborhood Story Project.

Introduction

My name is Kenneth Randel Phillips Martin. I grew up in the St. Bernard Housing Development in the Seventh Ward of New Orleans. Even though I haven't lived in "Dat B" since 2005, it remains a powerful force in my life. For the last few years, my family has lived in a duplex on Paris Avenue in the Seventh Ward. It's a big street, the houses are spread out, and we don't see our neighbors very often. Sometimes I miss all the noise of the project.

Some people probably thought living in the project was stupid, but it wasn't. In the St. Bernard, some of us had fun, some of us had no fun, but all of us had responsibilities. It was hard work living there.

Then came Katrina, and our family and the St. Bernard were scattered throughout the country. Our project were flooded. On September 2, 2005, a picture of my great-grandmother and great-aunt were on the cover of Time magazine with a headline that read, "American Tragedy."

Two years later I got the chance to tell more of the story, to go beyond the tragedy of what was lost. As I began writing this book, I decided to go back to the St. Bernard to reconnect with my memories. Walking through the abandoned courtyards, I never heard anything so quiet, but I could picture everything how it used to be. Fridays were hang-out days, when the courts were packed with people. On Saturdays, our neighbors would have block parties, a splash, or card games on the porch.

Walking around in 2007, I didn't feel right not saying, "Hi, how you doing?" But there wasn't anyone to greet. It's a hard thing to look back at, and as I stood in different spots, I caught flashbacks. I passed the spot where my Uncle Irvin was killed on February 26, 2001, and a bad feeling ran through me. In Gibson court, I could see my little brother playing football while I was sitting on the porch with Kobey, the best dog ever. I pictured him running down the stairs and my neighbor, Ms. Lewis, calling out, "Run Kobey! Run Kobey!"

With no one in the Project it felt like a big responsibility to tell the stories of what we lost and what we have held onto. I've always said I wanted to be my own boss, and writing a book is sort of like being that—no one is telling you what to say. At first, it's exciting, but then it's scary. What do I really want to say, what stories were worth writing down and seeking out? I wrote pages and pages in my journal trying to figure it out, and began to sign them, "The President." When I've been too bossy, my younger brother calls me that. It gave me the courage to explore my past, and to talk to my family.

The St. Bernard shaped me, but it was no longer home. I loved it, but had to admit to myself that even with all the good, it could also be a painful and isolating place. I needed to figure out how to write about my history, but also what was going on in my life since Katrina. I wasn't sure who I was anymore. I just felt angry.

When I worked on my book, I usually wrote something mean. The stories were about days full of fighting and fussing, and wanting to be alone. I walked the streets thinking. For a long time, I didn't write some of the most important stories because of this fear of how others would judge me and my stories.

I decided to do interviews with my family to learn more about our relationships, history and experiences in public housing. Everyone was really supportive of me writing this book because our family values creativity and education. From music, art, writing, cooking, and interpreting dreams, we have found ways to express ourselves.

I built this book around the conversations I had with my family. I will introduce you to six of the people I'm closest to in the world, and then share the interviews we did together. Woven through the conversations are stories that I've written about my own life. Talking to them gave me a chance to understand myself better. I had to face my anger management problems. I've looked at how young men have been loved and nurtured in my community, but also sometimes boxed in by ideas about what men are supposed to be. I've talked to my family about the men we have lost to violence to preserve their memory, but I also wanted to write the stories of the men in my life who still are shaping their own futures.

Sign,
President

1

Terrance Phillips, by Lindsey Darnell.

I. Interview with My Brother, Terrance "T-Smasher" Phillips

The game fanatic, my brother Terrance, is the oldest out of the three of us. He was born May 11, 1989, and was raised by my mother and father. He's known for ribbing any and everybody—everything that comes out of his mouth is funny. When I walk in the door from school, he'll go, "Here comes Eddie Murphy." Other days he calls me Anthony Anderson. And when I'm mad he calls me "Mad Dog."

What's it like living in a house with Terrance? He keeps the fun going. Sometimes he'll do this little dance where he moves his legs without his feet leaving the ground to crack my mother and me up. He really has bad nerves. Sometimes he'll just click out, especially if you're aggravating, like me. I know I have been through a lot, but it's nothing compared to Terrance's life story.

He sits down with me in the kitchen and tells me stories about the life he had before I knew what life was. A long time ago Terrance was sitting at my Grandma Loretta's kitchen table, eating fried chicken and waiting on my daddy. Terrance said he heard gunshots and started to panic. Somebody with a very deep voice started kicking and punching the door. He started to recognize the voice. It was my daddy hollering, "Terrance!" He struggled to open the door because his hands were greasy and it was hard to turn the doorknob. When the door finally opened, my father rushed him into the house as gunshots from a nine millimeter came in behind him, tearing up the kitchen. If you ask me, if it wasn't for Terrance, my daddy wouldn't be here today.

Terrance is a competitor. Playing games is his thing—name any game and he will beat you at it. Even games he has never played before. One time me, Terrance, Kimani, my mama and Dewayne all sat in Terrance's room playing Royal Rumble, a boxing video game. First up was my mama and me. I beat her in no less than 30 seconds. Then I took on Kimani and beat him in less that a minute, turned around and knocked out Dewayne.

My mama said, "Uh oh, Terrance's turn." He was known to be the best, but I thought I had a chance. He picked up his joystick and after a few punches I received the big K.O. I held a big stupid look on my face and I slammed the remote to the ground. My mama told me to go to my room. As I walked out, I was sure I hated him, and wanted revenge. "One day," I yelled, "you're gonna meet your match!"

I interviewed my brother at our house on Paris Avenue, sitting around the dining room table. We talked about growing up with Kimani and our friends in the St. Bernard, our time in Houston, and our attitude problems when we were younger. He brings out the crazy side of me and makes me laugh at anything—including myself.

Interview with Terrance

Kenneth: Should we begin?

Terrance: Yes, sir.

Kenneth: How did it feel to be raised at the St. Bernard?

Terrance: It was a struggle. It was hard. My mama had three children and she was just struggling. She only had one job housekeeping at the Quarter House—a hotel in the French Quarter, and she was off and on with it.

Kenneth: Who was your favorite person to hang out with in the St. Bernard and why?

Terrance: Oh, man. It was Ahyaro. We met at Nelson, our elementary school. You remember Mr. Knight and all them? You know, they had the classes go against other classes. I had to race Ahyaro, and I beat him—twice! We'd be cursing each other out. Come to find out he stayed in the same court, the same complex as me. We just started talking and we got cool. We started calling each other cousin. We used to fuss like real blood. He's the tallest one. He's six-foot ten-inches. I'm six-foot four-and-a-half inches.

Kenneth: What do you remember most about living in the St. Bernard?

Terrance: We could never go outside—only on Friday and Saturday, sometimes Sundays. And I felt like, "Everybody else outside. Why we can't go outside on the weekday?"

Kenneth: We couldn't do nothing, we had to stay upstairs—we could barely go on the porch sometimes.

Terrance: This is what we used to do. We used to have a little conversation between the three of us, and then while one of us went to ask our mom, we ducked so we could hear what she was about to say. She'd be like, "No! Get back inside!" But if I think about it now, I just laugh. If I asked my mama right now, "Why we had to stay inside, Ma?" "Because." That's her answer.

Kenneth: "I said so."

Terrance: "Because I'm your mama."

Kenneth: And they'd stay outside until six o'clock on a school day. Sunday you couldn't make an exit out that door.

Terrance: Because school's tomorrow.

Left: Terrance, Kenneth, and Kimani on their balcony in the St. Bernard. *Right:* Kenneth and his mother, Lynette. Photographs courtesy of Lynette Phillips.

Driveway in the St. Bernard, courtesy of Lynette Phillips.

The Weekend

Saturday, the middle of third grade. Another free day to go outside without my mom having to bother me. I walked on the porch and looked downstairs to see who was outside, and the bottom porch was filled with people.

I decided to put on some clothes and go outside. Before I could reach for the door knob, my mama said, "Where you going, Doodie?" I said, "Nowhere, I'm going in the court." I walked around to the driveway. I liked it because the kids always got to play in the streets. It was so hot outside. When I looked across the street, I saw a group of kids and their mama playing on a water slide. I asked if I could play too, because it looked like fun. She said, "Yeah, you could get in." I ran back upstairs to ask my mama.

She said, "Whose water slide?" I said, "The people across the street." She walked me over there after I changed into my swimming trunks. A boy my age, tall with a big head, finished running and sliding through the water. He walked over by me and said, "What's your name?" I said "Kenneth, why? What's yours?" He said, "Oh, I'm Keith. Do you want to take a turn on the slide?" I said, "Yeah," and from there we started being friends. He stayed across the street from me, and so we hung together everyday.

Keith lived with his mama Daphne, and his brother Brian, and sister Jana. He told me his daddy was dead, but we never talked about it. My dad had moved out the year before, but we didn't talk about that, either.

TOO CRAZY

Kenneth: What was it like being raised by our daddy? Well, like, you know, my daddy.

Terrance: Well, you should know, I've been through a lot with him—a lot. Growing up, my real daddy wasn't staying with us.

Kenneth: All right, what type of things did you like to do with daddy?

Terrance: He used to bring me places—bring me to the mall to go shopping. But the negative side, that was crazy. I can't forget none of that.

Kenneth: Like what?

Terrance: I went with him one day. He told my mama, "We're coming right back." I was young, so I didn't know where we were going. We get into some car, he goes and picks all his friends up. We're riding around and they robbed somebody. I didn't know what it was—I was just looking around inside the car, and we just drove off. The same night, the same dudes they robbed came back and found us. Our car was parked in the Eighth Ward at his brother's house. We were about to get out and they were coming from a block away, walking behind the car shooting.

I thought it was firecrackers until the windows started busting. And then your daddy got out of the car. He had to be shooting back, and he just shoulder bumped his brother's front door and broke it down. If he didn't, he would've gotten shot. Luckily, the dudes didn't walk up on the car, because I was still sitting in the car. Only thing I could do is duck. The bullet, when it hit the window, passed right by my head. Yeah. It was just a crazy life with him.

It wasn't my first time. My mama told me when I was a baby, a bullet ricocheted off the wall of Grandma's house and fell in the bed near my leg. These things I didn't know. I was small. It took for me to get at least seven years old to begin to understand. I used to be watching movies and the shoot-outs they had in the movies, he was doing.

Kenneth: How'd you feel when my daddy moved out in 2001?

Terrance: To me it got to the point where I didn't care—go ahead! Because it was like the same old thing. Every holiday, he and my mom were fussing.

Kenneth: Or fighting.

Terrance: He'd be sleeping out on the porch, sleeping in the car. Got a whole house. You got a home. I don't know, that's what drugs do to you. She could have left him.

Kenneth: But he was too crazy.

Terrance: Yeah, he really was. Back then, he was nothing to be played with, but she just kept giving him chances. And he kept repeating and doing the same old thing.

He's about his business. Back then you couldn't fuss with him either, you'd get punched down. He hit too hard. You couldn't tell him nothing. When it came to war, he was like a soldier. If you were talking about shooting, he's got guns. He had more than one. He fought like a boxer. Couldn't beat him. That's where you get your attitude from. You don't let nobody play with you.

Killa Kenneth Kane

In our household, my father was known as Daddy. On the streets, he was given the name Killa Kenneth Kane. His friends called me Lil Kane and they gave Kimani the name Killa. One day, when I was in kindergarten, I watched my daddy run in and out the door, switching gun after gun. My daddy turned around when he heard Kimani move a chair from behind him. He smacked him and made him go in the room by himself. We never liked being sent to our room. It was just too dark. I ran behind Kimani to keep him company. As soon as I made it to the room, I heard six guns going off at one time. Kimani and I jumped in the closet. My heart was racing. I held my little brother's hand so tight. When I let go we both were sweating.

Our mom ran in the room screaming "Doodie! Moonie!" We were in the closet covered in our mama and daddy's clothes. When she found us she took us in to the living room with Terrance. She put us on the sofa. She was crying, which made Kimani and me cry. We hate to see our mother down. The last thing I heard her say was, "No matter what, I will always be there for y'all." She cried even harder. My heart stumbled. I worried that she was in danger.

One time she set us down at the kitchen table and she asked us, "Do y'all think me and your daddy should get married?" She asked us all ten times. Kimani and Terrance were saying yes and maybe, but all my answers were "No!"

I just couldn't picture my parents being married. I don't think things would go right. Some days they put a smile on me and my brothers' faces, but we already knew how things would go down. At the end of the day, the two wound up fussing and fighting. Kimani would hear them and go knock on their door, crying. I'd wake up and try to stop them. When they separated in 2000, it was a big relief on my brothers and me.

Kenneth cooking in the St. Bernard, courtesy of Irma Phillips.

BROTHERS

Kenneth: What was it like living across the street from Grandma Irma?

Terrance: Oh, man, that was fun cause I know once my mama made groceries, we couldn't really touch them. We couldn't touch nothing. I mean, we couldn't open the icebox.

Kenneth: I used to sneak and do it.

Terrance: I'm glad my grandma stayed close to me because when I was thirsty, I would run to her house.

Kenneth: We couldn't even touch a cold drink! I used to be dying to go to school because, you know, free water!

Terrance: For real.

Kenneth: She didn't play at all. And then if she cooks and we don't eat it, she'll say, "I ain't cooking no more!"

Terrance: When we eat it——

Kenneth: "Damn! Y'all ate every damn thing up!" I'd be like, "Oh my God."

Terrance: But now you cook for real. Back then it was chili and eggs.

Kenneth: Terrence, I made that for me. That wasn't for y'all.

Terrance: But still—that doesn't go together.

Kenneth: I would cook breakfast, though.

Terrance: Boy, no you didn't.

Kenneth: I learned to cook biscuits and eggs and all that—

Terrance: No, you just did that. That was last weekend.

Kenneth: No, I'm talking about in the project. I wasn't doing that?

Terrance: No. That ain't hard!

Kenneth: Shut up, Terrance! [*Laughter*] What's it like to grow up with two younger brothers?

Terrance: I'm gonna break it down. I'm never bored. I can mess with y'all all day. Wrestle, play video games, walk around the block.

Kenneth: How are Kimani and I different?

Terrance: All right. Well you, you're attitude. Sometimes nobody can't tell you nothin. You act older than your age. Like, how can I really put it? You're an old man in a young person's body. Kimani, he's in his own world. Kimani don't really mess with nobody. Kenny, when you sing, you're loud. You'll come all in my ear. Another thing, you'll put your hand in my face and start out with, "First of all." You'll say that ten times and then launch into, "Long as you don't touch me!"

Kenneth: That's down bad. [*Laughter*]

Terrance: You and me could talk about anything. We hardly fuss. If we do fuss, it's over something stupid like a computer. You're a MySpace head. If I'm on the computer before you and you want to get on, you'll get mad and walk out of the house.

Another thing you'll do—you're nosey. If I'm on the phone, and you'll be like, "Who that is? Huh? Huh, Terrance?" I'm just like, "Don't worry about that." You're like, "I'm just asking! Lord!"

But I'm a comedian. If I'm bored and you're on the phone, it's my turn to aggravate you. I'll start clowning you. You get mad and be like, "That ain't funny. That ain't funny." I just keep messing with you til you get drove.

Kenneth: I laugh sometimes, though. Do you have any funny stories to share about us growing up?

Terrance: All right. Pictures. We have some pictures we just laugh at. They have a picture of us in this bunk bed with no clothes on. You are throwing the peace sign up, and me too, like we don't know what we're doing. And we laugh at that every time.

Kenneth: How about the time I skipped summer school that day? I was like, "Should I cut?" I wanted to go to the pool. Kimani was like, "Yeah, go ahead then." At the pool, I was standing by the deep end, and I can't swim. This dude just pushed me into the

Terrance, Kenneth, and Kimani, courtesy of Lynette Phillips.

10

water and I went to flopping and kicking. I was getting ready to drown until my friend Charles came and just grabbed me out of the pool.

Then I made it home, and the counselor had called my mama. Mama asked me, "Why wasn't you at school?" I was like, "Yes, I was." I had everything prepared. I had done some homework on my way home from the pool. She asked Kimani, "Did Kenneth go to school? And he was like, "Yeah, yeah… No, he didn't." And, Lord!

Terrance: Yeah, I was right there when you caught a whupping. [*Laughter*] I got another one. Remember when we were coming back from walking my girl home, and Kimani was riding a bike in front of us. It was dark, and I told him be careful, but he hit something and flipped over the bike—slow.

Kenneth: Everything went in the air and it was like slow motion. [*Laughter*] He fell without a scratch.

Terrance: And running after our dog. Kobey was so intelligent. We'd leave him on the porch on the third floor and he'll find some way to unleash himself and go all the way down the steps and run around the whole project.

Kenneth: And we had to chase him!

Terrance: And by me being the fastest, they'd call a hero alert for me to go find him.

Kenneth: I couldn't catch him.

Terrance: And he was strong.

Kenneth: Unless I had some food or something.

Terrance: He had the whole court just running after him. He was just dodging every one of them.

Kenneth: Everybody would jump on him and try to get him, but he would—

Terrance: Just be gone. He looked like a lion running. A fox or something.

Kobey

Back in the St. Bernard days, some old friends of my parents moved downstairs from us. Their names were Ms. Tandra and Mr. Grey. They had this dog named C-grams who gave birth to a litter of puppies just before school was out for the summer. My mom had planned on getting a puppy. I said, "Lord, please let her get us a dog," and my prayer was answered. Out of the eight puppies that C-grams had, my mom asked for a special one. We named him after our first dog, Kobey, because they looked so much alike. They both had a pretty brown coat and beige tail.

He was unbelievable. He was our hallway guard dog. Every time he heard someone put their foot on the first step, he would bark. We would sit on the porch together. Well, at first we had to tie his lil bad ass up or he would go run downstairs. I remember one time when he was a baby, Terrance used to come in the hallway with him on his shoulders.

We didn't look at Kobey as a dog. We looked at him as one of us. He always ate table food. He didn't want to eat his food unless he didn't see us eat. One time, I made some hot dogs for him and me. Then I sat on the porch and ate them all. My mama came up the court and hollered, "Kobey!" Kobey jumped in the window and was all excited to see her. She came up the stairs and gave him a hug and said she was hungry. She looked in the kitchen and said, "Who ate Mama's hot dogs?" I wasn't going to say anything, but Kobey looked at me and barked.

When the hurricane hit New Orleans, I was by my grandmother's house in the St. Bernard. A boat came

Kenneth and Kimani with Kobey, courtesy of Lynette Phillips.

to take us to the bridge. I saw someone throw their puppy off the bridge and some people were just letting their dogs run loose. I was separated from my mother and brothers for a long time, and it wasn't a good feeling. My mom told me later, before she left the house, they gave Kobey a big hug and kiss. A lot of tears were shed. My grandma Irma, my cousins, great aunts, and I moved to Richard, Louisiana. It looked like the country. I wanted to find my mother and brothers.

One day, I came home from school and my cousin LaLa told me that my grandmother had to tell me something. I'm thinking it's something good. She looked at me and held my hand. She said, "Leslie went back to y'all's house and found Kobey dead." I couldn't breathe. It was like the end of the world to me. I cried and cried. Losing him was a shock to me. It hurt to know he died without us there. I could still picture him coming home and just going back to chilling like we used to, but he was gone.

ATTITUDE PROBLEM

Kenneth: What elementary school did you go to?

Terrance: Medard H. Nelson Elementary. As a matter of fact, it's down the street from the house I stay in now, on Paris Avenue at St. Bernard.

Kenneth: What do you remember most about it?

Terrance: Just going to school, doing my work. I wasn't bad until I got in sixth grade, and I done grew dreadlocks! [*Laughter*] It's like I turned into another person when I got dreadlocks. My cousin attended with me, so we stayed in trouble. The week before graduation, this dude still had one of my video games. I caught him in the hallway one morning. I was like, "Where's my game?" He was like, "Man, I'm not finished with it." I'm like, "Man, I need my game." I asked him one more time, "So you ain't gonna give my game?" He was like, "No." I'm like, "Oh yeah?" I had a wrapped up peanut butter and jelly cracker and I smashed it all in his face. I smashed it everywhere. I didn't care. Ms. Hoffman took mug shots of his face.

I had an attitude. I just thought it was cool, but it wasn't. I thought I was gaining respect for that. People was like, "Dang, Terrance left his haircut for dreads. He done went crazy like." You couldn't tell me nothing. One time I started a fight on purpose. I was eating lunch and had this dude looking at me. I grew up with him. I got up. I grabbed him by his shirt, and I was slamming him to the wall. I slammed him on the floor. He was trying to fight back, but I picked him up. I was about to punch him, and I just stopped.

My sixth grade teacher, Ms. Dean, knew how I was. If I'm getting into it with somebody, she'll bring me outside to talk to me. I'd be like, "Man, I'm not really caring what you're saying."

She'd ask, "Why you have that attitude?"

I'm like, "It's just the way I feel."

She'd be like, "How do you feel?"

I'm like, "I don't know. I can't explain it." I was full of rage. It was just my attitude problem. I calmed it because I noticed it wasn't worth it.

Terrance at school, courtesy of Irma Phillips.

Kenneth: When did you realize that being funny could be a better way of going through the world than being angry?

Terrance: Like me being funny?

Kenneth: Yes, sir.

Terrance: I feel like if you don't know how to do anything, you're nothing. You got to learn how to do something at least! That kept my day going, me joking around instead of being mad. But I wasn't funny at first. I didn't know what a joke was until I started hanging around the dudes that stayed in the same building as me, and I got better than them. I was the youngest one, and I just stuck with it.

Kenneth: Morris was the skinniest—

Terrance: He's older than me. Weighed like 80 pounds. He can't wear a hat on his head—pysche, no! He's got a small head.

Kenneth: They used to be on the bike—Morris on the back, and New Jack would be riding—around the project calling everybody "Egghead Ass!" It'd be funny.

Terrance: It's so easy to get in drama down here for anybody—by looking at them. I know it's time for a change, but that ain't changing. Who you know gonna change it? Al Sharpton? New Orleans is ignorant. The violence is crazy. Know what I'm talking about Kenneth?

Kenneth: Yeah.

Terrance: You've been in so many fights. Out of all my mama's children, you fought the most. Got into it mostly every other day. You can't tell you nothing, just like your daddy. You look exactly like your daddy! I done watched your daddy fight. You get it from your daddy—the attitude is crazy when he fights.

Anger Management

Punk, sissy, fag, you name it, Keith and I heard it all before, but I didn't take nothing from nobody.

One day we got into a fuss with our neighbor Sheila Fields' grandson, Wayne.

Keith, Willie and I were walking down the drivewa. Wayne was in the hallway window, and called out, "Look at that punk right there."

I said, "Who you talking to?"

Willie said, "Come downstairs."

Keith took off his shirt as Wayne came downstairs and said, "What, fag?"

Willie said, "Get him, Keith."

Keith didn't make a move, so I did it for him. Keith jumped in and started stomping Wayne. Keith said, "Who a fag now?"

Willie's mama, Lanita, screamed for my mama and she came to window.

"Girl, Keith, Lil Kenneth, and Willie was fighting Ms. Sheila's children."

My mama came downstairs and said, "Why y'all was fighting?"

Willie said, "Because he called us fags."

My mama said, "Y'all had the right to fight him. Who hit who first?"

We got quiet.

Lanita said, "Who hit who?"

I said, "I hit him first."

My mama said, "Why Doodie?"

Keith said, "Because he was walking up on us."

I said, "I just wasn't going to stand there."

My mama said, "Well, y'all know what? All y'all stay right here." She made us sit down until we came to our senses.

We walked up the court. Willie turned around, because he heard Ms. Sheila fussing at Wayne: "Go sit downstairs and I dare somebody to play with you." And yes, of course, Keith opened his mouth. He said, "We advise you to not let him downstairs. If you do he's going to get his ass beat again."

Wayne said, "Don't play with my grandma!" and Willie countered, "Oh, so now you hard? Man, come downstairs. I'ma show you what I'm talking about."

I think my mama had heard enough, and yelled from our balcony, "Doodie, bring your ass upstairs, all ya'll!" Willie ran as fast as he could up the stairs, and I was right behind him.

Wayne said, "Punk asses…"

MUSIC IN OUR FAMILY

Kenneth: What kind of music do you listen to?

Terrance: I listen to rap and R&B.

Kenneth: What's your most favorite though?

Terrance: It's hard cause they got a lot of R&B that's better than rap. It probably doesn't seem like that to you because I'm always rapping around you. But last night I was listening to Genuine.

Kenneth: Whitney Houston.

Terrance: Man, I don't like her, man!

Kenneth: I do.

Terrance: Psyche! She's cool, but—you know what I'm about to say? When I'm about to go to sleep, you'll go on YouTube and replay that same video over and over til I'll want to throw water on the computer. That's aggravating.

Kenneth: "Exhale." That's my song.

Terrance: Speaking of bounce, bounce ain't the same no more. DJ Jubilee and those dudes could do regular dances. Catch a bounce song now. You're gonna see girls with their heads doing Olympic tricks and all that. The beats are a lot faster.

Kenneth: I like some of it. When they play an R&B song and put a bounce beat to it.

Terrance: People back then used to make their own bounce songs up. They got people that still do that, but a lot just take a popular song and put a bounce beat to it, say like Beyonce's "Ego." But New Orleans got its own style. If you bring a bounce CD to Canada, people are gonna just look at you like, "What is this?"

Now see, when I go other places, they like our accent. I hear the same thing, "You mixed with African and Jamaican?" Because of my accent. The way we talk—we don't talk like nobody else. We got our own slangs.

Kenneth: What do you remember about our uncle Irvin?

Terrance: I just know he was a known DJ. He'd been locked up for eight years. There was not too much to remember about him.

Kenneth: I didn't know him. I just knew he was my mama's brother. The day I met him, he had an S-curl in his head and he had a big old smile. I don't know who he was. She just always told us about him. We had a picture of him at his wedding—black and white.

Terrance: Yeah, he came back in 2000. I was happy to see him, though. He wasn't out no longer than two months. He used to come by my mama's house a couple of times. He'd keep his headphones on and come to see us. Back then, he had a face like, *oooh*, that boy looked crazy! He had golds in his mouth. He was crazy about our mama.

Kenneth: One time, you punched this girl in the chest at school.

Terrance: Oh yeah! I hit the girl hard. That's why I say I'm not the same. I don't hit females, but back then I had a mind like, "Don't play with me. Don't tell me nothing. Don't disrespect me." I made two girls cry. My mama must have called my uncle. This

Uncle Irvin at his wedding, courtesy of Irma Phillips.

is how it happened: We're playing a game.

Kenneth: I was beating some drumsticks.

Terrance: He was so mean when he was mad. He came in the room, "Turn that game off!" You beating with the drum: "Give me the sticks!"

Kenneth: I was scared. I backed up and everything.

Terrance: He tells me, "Punch me like you hit the girl." I know how I hit the girl. I cocked back and hit her, but I tapped him. And boom! He punched me and I flew. Then he was on his son Brandon's case for getting suspended. He said, "You give my sister and your mother one more problem, I'm gonna break your nose." But I wish he was still living. The day of his funeral, that's the day he was supposed to DJ at the St. Bernard Center. He was about to blow up or something. The last time I seen him before he died, he was acting strange.

Kenneth: I know. I thought the same thing.

Terrance: He looked the same but he didn't act the same. That whole day he didn't say one word. None! He didn't say hey, hi—nothing. When he died, I was just like, "Oh, all right, we're gonna have a repass." It was packed. That was the whole project. And it was cold out there, too.

Kenneth: The street was closed off.

Terrance: The stores stayed open late and people had his memorial shirt on.

Kenneth: His son Brandon was on the mike rapping.

Terrance: You celebrate it, you know what I'm saying? It's sad that he's gone but I felt good around that time. Like, "Dang, all these people came." He had mad love.

EVACUATION

Kenneth: What did you think when the project flooded and you had to leave without me?

Terrance: I didn't care. Psyche! That was crazy. I was wondering where you went when everybody got on different buses. I wasn't with my mama, I was with Ahyaro in the Astrodome. Then Ahyaro and them went to Virginia, so I was by myself. You was in Lafayette. Kimani and Mama in Houston. It didn't feel right because we weren't together. Somebody said, "Man, I just seen your mama." I'm like, "Where at?"

Kenneth: I had no clue where anybody was. Phones weren't working.

Terrance: If you stayed, you were gonna suffer. A thousand people on Causeway in Metarie. Mud. Wet mud at that. I didn't go to sleep. I fought my sleep.

Kenneth: I remember I had the same clothes on for the longest. I had a different pair of underwear and everything, but I had the same clothes on. I found this Calvin Klein jumper and I had to wear that all day. I didn't have nothing!

Terrance: No drawers or nothing.

Kenneth: Yes I did! Yes, I did have drawers. You used to clown me about my jumper all the time. It was name brand.

August 29, 2005

It was around four-thirty in the evening. It was my brothers, my mom, Dewayne, my uncle Irvin's son Brandon, Kobey, and me at home. My mama gave everybody something to do. She made Kimani fill every container up with water, Terrance had to throw away all of the trash, and Brandon and I had to walk Kobey outside.

I jumped up off the sofa and said, "Come on, Kobey." I walked toward the door and he ran toward his leash. I said, "Get it" and he grabbed the leash from the top of the fish tank and brought it to me. About the time we made it outside, it was getting dark and the winds were picking up real quick. As we walked, the wind was pushing us back. I asked Brandon, "Can you hold onto Kobey for a minute while I tie my shoes?" I turned around and that fool wasn't anywhere to be found. Kobey had run off again. We found him in the field in the back of our driveway, cornering a bird.

When we got back home, I called my grandma Irma to see what she was doing, but she didn't pick up the phone. Brandon and I decided to go over to visit her. It was my two great aunts: Clarrisa and Olive, my uncle Richard, and my three cousins: La'Chanae, lil aggravating Lathan, and my cousin Chanqual. We sat in my grandma's living room and were talking. My mama called and told my grandma it was time for us to come back across the street.

Brandon Phillips, courtesy of the Irma Phillips.

The rain had started coming down too hard and we had to stay at my grandma Irma's house. The lights went out and we stayed up with flashlights, laughing until the grown ups came in and made us go to sleep.

In the morning, I woke up to a breeze coming in the bedroom window. It felt good and I thought the worst was over. I put on my slippers to go back by my mama. When I walked in the kitchen where everybody was, my grandma said, "Where you think you going?" I said, "I'm about to get ready to go home." She said, "Go look outside." Her driveway was filled with almost eight feet of brown water with trash and gasoline in it.

Next door to us, Ms. Thelma and her family had slept outside on the porch because it was so hot. I saw people on their porches waving red and white shirts every time a helicopter passed. People hammering holes through their roofs. People throwing their refrigerators off of their railings so they would be able to float across the water. Others were putting their kids in inflatable pools and on top of plywood, getting in the water and pushing them.

Mr. Bryant, who stayed across the court with his wife and his son Lil Bryant, had the biggest boat. Kimani and I used to play with Lil Bryant when he didn't have anybody to play with. After he got his family out of the water, he started to help other families. He asked if we needed any help and my grandma said, "No thank you. We are waiting for the National Guard to come. We have been waiting a while for them to come."

When they finally came, they told us we couldn't have so many bags—only one or two. Well, I didn't have any bags. A matter of fact, all I had was the clothes I already had on, but I held all my grandma's bags for her. I had to jump from the steps and take a big leap into the boat. It was my first time ever being in one.

It was sad to see the project just sink like that. I didn't know where we were going, and I was hoping to see my mama and brothers, but when we got to the 610 bridge, there wasn't any sign of them.

The bridge was packed with people and helicopters picking people off the bridge. We found a spot and my uncle Richard, my cousin Brandon, and I went to look for my mama and my brothers. My mama's boyfriend, Dewayne, found us and said he had been separated from them when they got on the boats.

We waited a couple of hours. Some helicopters were dropping big boxes of food in packages with candy and mints. To make the food hot, we had to put water and food inside a bag, close it and then let the water boil. It tasted good considering it was food coming from plastic bags. There were people out there with their babies—some of the babies were newborns who didn't have anything to eat because their mothers had run out of formula.

The buses showed up around 1:00 a.m., and it was freezing outside. As the buses began to load with people, my grandma and my aunts were in the back of the line asking me and my cousins to save them seats next to us. People were fighting to get on the bus. I couldn't think of anything but my mama and brothers. As the bus drove off, we passed up people still standing on the bridge, crying and begging for help.

It was like ten degrees on that bus. Everybody was cold and all I had on was what we call a beater—a tank top—and some shorts with a pair of slippers. My grandma gave me one of her towels she had in a bag. I fell asleep and woke up at a McDonald's, where I met up with my fourth grade music teacher, Mrs. Shanks. She tapped me on my shoulder while she was getting off the bus and said, "Do you remember me?" I looked at my grandma and my grandma said, "I'm not the one that's talking," so I looked back at Mrs. Shanks and said "No." She said, "You don't? You used to love coming to my class. Your favorite song to sing was 'Oh, Happy Day.'" I do like that song, but I couldn't remember her for nothing in the world. Then she just said, "I'm Mrs. Shanks." My grandma said, "Uh oh, you never know who knows you."

Everybody came out of McDonald's. We were back on the road, and I was back to sleep. I was tired from staying on that bridge. The next time I woke up, we were in front of "The Cajun Dome" in Lafayette, Louisiana. At least ten to 20 thousand people were outside. There were so many people that they started taking some to Texas.

Before we could go in, they searched us at the door. Then we had to go find a spot. We went to the very top where there wasn't anybody, and met up with my cousins. Dre'nell said she spotted my uncle Richard's head from a mile away.

My cousin Lathan and I helped them move their stuff right by ours. Nell's eyes were so red they looked like they caught fire. Her mother, my aunt Clarissa, walked her downstairs to the medical area. It was about time to take a shower but Brandon and I didn't have a change of clothes. Lathan gave us some and Nell found a clothing center in the arena right next door. She came back with a Calvin Klein jumper, two pairs of jeans, and three belts. Since I didn't have anything to wear at all, she gave me the jumper.

Before Dewayne left, he gave me a couple of shirts because that's all he had. He said he was going to Baton Rouge to find my mother and my brothers, but they were in Texas.

II. Interview with My Brother, Kimani Phillips

I didn't how know he got here, but this lil dude my mother gave birth to on June 22, 1993 is my best friend. My Aunt Loren named him "Kimani Eman." The name comes from Kenya. Not many people in our family call him by his full name. We usually say "Mani" or "Moonie." Together, Terrance and Ahyaro used to call us, "The Brothers of Destruction."

When we were little, we made a hut in our room out of the bed covers. We called it "Ilulu." We went into the kitchen and stole marshmallows, cookies, cold drinks, and cereal and went into the circle to talk about everything. It didn't have to be serious, but we covered what happened and what we wished would happen.

We were up in there for hours. Inside, we had different spaces—a living room, kitchen, and bedroom. Nobody could step in the Ilulu except for us and Kobey. If there was something we needed to discuss and didn't want to talk about it in front of the rest of our family, we would say, "Ilulu," and run into the bedroom to make the circle. And if we were mad at each other, one of us would say, "So you want to fight?" We made the Ilulu and fought on our knees. Our rule was we couldn't stand up. We felt safe there. It was our palace.

We made a pledge: "We (Doodie and Moonie) swear to never discuss any Ilulu business out of the Ilulu. If one of us does so, he will get the plunger stuck to his booty."

One time we took each other to court in the Ilulu and Kobey was our judge. We took off the head of a mop and taped it to Kobey's head and pled our case. Our lawyers were our teddy bears. Kimani called Kobey "Your Hugeness" and I addressed him, "Mister." He barked and sentenced both of us. We set up a camera like People's Court and Kobey, dressed in a blazer, interviewed us about the verdict. I thought I won the case and Kimani swore to God he won.

My lil brother is my backbone—the person I'm closest to in the world. He's generous, kind, smart in math, and does some stupid things that keep me laughing. One time I walked out of my room and he was ironing his clothes in the dining room, naked. He's uninhibited and doesn't care what other people think. When he meets you, he'll stare at you. Sometimes I tell him, "Stop looking at people like that," but he catches on to them real quick. He can do impressions of anyone: "Bra-man" from the T.V. show Martin, Whoopi Goldberg in *Sister Act II*, and our mama and daddy.

When we decided to do this interview, I already knew how he was going to act. I told him to be comfortable, but he kept things proper. I asked him about how he felt about our relationship with our daddy and talked to him about how I worried that he was trying too much to be a gangsta. He has a different perspective on things than I do. It's always good to hear how he feels. It reminded me of our Ilulu days.

Kimani Phillips, by Kenneth Phillips.

Kenneth: What's it like to grow up with two older brothers?

Kimani: It ain't really nothing but just having older role models, and people to tell me to go the right way or don't go the wrong way—don't be a follower but a leader.

Kenneth: That's it?

Kimani: Yeah.

Kenneth: So what type of things did you do with your brothers?

Kimani: You know, we used to be knocking on people's doors and running. They'd come outside and all of us would rat on each other, but we'll still be cool the next minute.

Kenneth: You rat on me a lot.

Kimani: No, it was the other way around.

Kenneth: No, it's you who rat on me a lot.

Kimani: Other way around.

Kenneth: One time, some of y'all dared me to go punch somebody's window. I punched the glass and my hand went straight through. A man inside was like, "Who the hell is that?" He came out on the porch with a shotgun, and we all just ran. [*Laughter*]

Kimani: Mhm. I used to hate staying inside a lot, but after we got the dog, Kobey, we used to just play with our dog and mess with him all day. We used to run in our room and he'd jump in the bed with us.

Kenneth: We would chase him with the vacuum cleaner. He used to run from it.

Kimani: And we used to be around the fire escape, and my mama never wanted us out there—we used to be lowering the ladder down to the ground and—

Kenneth: The weights would bring us back up high, high, high in the air.

Kimani in the doorway to the apartment in the St. Bernard, courtesy of Lynette Phillips.

Kimani: One time you slipped on a banana peel and rammed your head into the dumpster. [*Laughter*] And then you started screaming.

Kenneth: What were some of your good memories from the St. Bernard?

Kimani: Playing football in the court, playing baseball in the court, walking my dog all around the court, and walking by Mr. Joe's truck in the front of our door. He used to be selling candy, chips, cigarettes, snacks, juice, and cold drinks.

Shopping

Every time I think about this story I laugh:

One night, my mama sent my dad to Winn-Dixie with Kimani and me to pick up a few things for the house. When we got there, Kimani and I wanted to wear his extra large white t-shirts that were in the car. The shirts came down to our ankles. Kimani's shirt was dragging on the ground. In the store, we ran straight for the candy section. My daddy said, "Bring y'all big head asses here. I'm not buying candy for y'all." We followed him all the way by the cold drinks, then we turned around and ran by the cookies.

We took a pack of vanilla and chocolate cookies off the shelf, ran by the working scrubs, opened the box and started eating them. We couldn't eat them fast enough because we were too busy laughing at each other. When we finished, we ran to the front of the store. When our dad spotted us, he had a real mean face on him. We tried not to laugh, but we couldn't help it. When he got out of the line, he said, "If anybody ask, y'all are not my children."

He started laughing, and we knew we were caught. We forgot to wipe the crumbs from around our mouths, plus we had melted chocolate on his shirts.

OUT OF THE WINDOW

Kenneth: What are the struggles our family went through and how did we overcome them?

Kimani: The struggles were putting groceries on the table, getting food for our dog, getting clothes and shoes for school, and having to stack up all my great grandma's stuff to put her in the old folk's home—that was a lot of struggle for my grandma.

Kenneth: Do you remember when you took the fall—the out-the-window fall?

Kimani: Oh! Well, in St. Bernard, when I was young, I didn't know what I was doing, and I pushed the screen to look and see where my brother and them were at, and I just fell out of the window. I don't even remember it, though.

Kenneth: I remember. Mama wouldn't let you outside so you was acting crazy, pushing your head through the screen. I didn't see you actually fall out the window, but I saw you flipping and hit the pole. Your head was bleeding. Mama flew down the steps.

Kimani: And my mama said, when she looked back, the screen was gone. I was screaming?

Kenneth: Yeah! Yes, indeed! You were on the ground, face down. I jumped off the porch, and I wanted to come grab for you, but people were holding me back.

Kimani: I didn't hit the pole, huh?

Kenneth: Yes, indeed, you hit the pole.

Kimani: I don't remember none of that.

Kimani's Fall

I remember sitting in the hospital next to Terrance, asking him, "Is Kimani going to die?" with tears running down my face. He had to stay in the hospital for a couple of days. My first visit, I had a fruit basket for him. My mama came out of the room and said, "Come here, Doo." I got out of my chair in the waiting room and walked slowly toward her. She grabbed my hand and walked me in.

Kimani was standing up. He looked at me, and I started crying. My mama picked me up and put me in the bed with him. He pointed at the fruit basket and gave me a picture he colored for me. It was a picture of Barney and BJ.

Boy, was I happy when he came home. Everywhere he went, I went. That's just the way we were when we were little. The only thing that mattered was that he was okay.

I became his protector. My brother is my everything. I can't stand to see him hurt by something or someone. That's how I've always been, and I don't think I'll ever change. My family doesn't like to talk about the fall because people will say he's slow and he's far from it. He just sometimes answers questions slow. From being around him so much, I can usually predict when those times will come.

For awhile, my mama brought the fall up too much, and one day Kimani walked off. I walked off with him, saying, "Nobody wants to hear about that all the time."

NONE OF US LEFT OUT

Kenneth: Do you remember the day in the park with Willie?

Kimani: Yeah.

Kenneth: Tell me about some of those days.

Kimani: I just seen Willie today. He was riding on a bike going toward Robert E. Lee. I was on my bus, but we can't holler out the window. I was just listen-ing to my iPod. I don't really talk on the bus when I have something to listen to.

Kenneth: What were you listening to?

Kimani: B.G. and Soulja Slim, sometimes T.I. and Lil Wayne. But yeah, it used to be me, you, Willie, Keith, Eugene, and sometimes Steve. We did a lot of things together when we were young. Every time we'd go walk places, none of us were left out.

Willie Hall Park, by Abram Himelstein.

Day of Freedom

A day at Willie Hall Park is a day of freedom. Sometimes Kimani, Willie, Keith, Kimani's best friend Eugene, and I got on our bikes and rode to the park at the back of the project near the bayou. Willie grew up with four sisters and one little brother. He lost his father years ago, but he still had his mother Lavita, and grandmother, Ms. Cynthia. Eugene's mama, Leslie, and our mama were best friends, too.

The only thing I didn't like was riding on that bumpy street—Milton. When we got to the park, everybody would race to the only two swings. Sometimes they would fight because one person would stay on the swing too long.

Old dudes stayed on the basketball court all the time. They thought we were afraid of them, but we showed them. One time, one of the older dudes walked by us and told Kimani to get off the swing. I was like, "My brother's not going nowhere."

He said, "Who you talking to, lil bitch?"

Kimani was like, "Don't talk to my brother like that, before it be something."

The old dude walked back to the basketball court. All of us pimped on the toys. Everybody had their own lil spot. I sat on the slide and looked at the older dudes who were just silhouettes in the sunlight. I turned around and was like, "Y'all, I got an idea."

Kimani said, "What Doodie? I hope it ain't stupid like the last time we tried to go to the bayou and steal some turtles."

I said, "It ain't that stupid of an idea. I still have the five dollars Mama gave me. Do you have yours?"

"Why? You ain't getting it."

"Let's go to the store and get some eggs."

For some nine and ten year olds, we did good. As we rode to Spider's Store, everybody was quiet. I went in the back to get the eggs and when I went up to the counter to buy them, a man that worked there said, "I know y'all not going home with these eggs." I said, "Why not?"

He started laughing and said, "If I catch eggs on my car I'ma kick y'all ass." He had a little slob coming out his mouth from laughing so much and had to wipe his mouth.

By the time we got back to the park, the older dudes were sitting on the bleachers. We dropped our bikes by the gate slowly so they wouldn't hear us. Kimani threw the first egg and it landed on one of the dudes' legs. He looked up like he thought it had come from a bird, and then we all started throwing them, before running out of the gate, and jumping on our bikes. They said, "We're going to get y'all," but we were already off with our middle fingers up in the sky.

BIGGEST FAN

Kenneth: What do you remember about living near Grandma?

Kimani: You know, just a lot of good things. I went to church with my grandma a lot. She'd be reading about the Lord, and having me answer questions about when the Lord was living, why they obeyed Him or disobeyed Him. She helped me out a lot with school projects.

Kenneth: What about that whupping?

Kimani: Well, I remember she embarrassed me. Like I had an audience coming up to the porch, and she hit me with a stick.

Kenneth: What made her do that?

Kimani: Me not following my mama's words about not staying outside while she's at work.

Kenneth: I ran. Do you remember when Uncle Irvin came home?

Kimani: Yeah. When I first saw my uncle Irvin in person, he dapped me off. He was like, "Boy, y'all got big." Half of our family came by my grandma's house to see my uncle. He started rapping, and talking to us about how we had been doing in school. He was really good at DJing and drawing.

Kenneth: You remember that day he started DJing and bucked you up to rap and dance?

Kimani: Yeah.

Kenneth: Like, tell about that moment, please.

Kimani: I went by my uncle's house up in New Orleans East. He showed us everything. He was DJing in front of us. Like even when he was in the project by my grandma's house, he used to be DJing. And every time I walked in the room by him, he had headphones on his head and he was mixing. He was about to sign with—who was Uncle Irv about to sign with, Cash Money?

Kenneth: Somebody. You was in a magazine before. In *Da R.U.D.E.* there's a picture of you and one of your favorite rappers, B.G.

Kimani: Yeah. My daddy called me out of the car. I didn't know who it was. My daddy was like, "This the B.G." He was like, "What's happening, lil wardie?" I dapped him off, and I couldn't believe it was B.G., my favorite rapper! I took pictures with him. Actually, that was my daddy's cousin's best friend.

My aunt wrote, "B.G. and his biggest fan, Kimani" in the magazine. That's how a lot of people know me in the St. Bernard. They used to be calling me, "Boy, that was you in the magazine?"

Kenneth: Loren's a writer, and she published a lot of things in her magazine *Da R.U.D.E.* She interviewed rappers like Lil Wayne. She interviewed Mia X, all of them.

Kimani: That's her best friend.

Kenneth: She was like one of my favorite rappers when I was growing up.

Kimani: I never actually get to hear her music unless my mama plays it.

Kenneth: Who were your favorite people in the St. Bernard?

Kimani: My cousin, Messy Man, who died, his real name was Alfred Edwards. He was like one of my best cousins on my daddy's side. Everything I used to be whining over, like belt buckles and wave caps, he'd give to me. He took me to the teen club.

Kenneth: The Rising Sun.

Kimani: I was only nine years old, and you had to be 13 to get in. You had to have a stamp on your arm, and I got in free. He took me to ride with him when I used to be, like, "I wanna go with you." He took me to the Gentilly Fair when I was around eight.

Messy Man

Even though my parents broke up, my aunts and cousins on my father's side still look at my mom as their sister-in-law and aunt. Especially Messy Man. He watched us when we were little and kept us laughing. He did this little dance on one leg, with one arm over his head. I got hooked on it, too. He dressed up in our clothes just to make fun of us. One time, he slept on the pillow that Kobey peed on, but me and my brothers didn't know until we woke up and saw his face smashed in the pillow. We all started laughing— even Kobey. The way his tongue was hanging out his mouth, it looked like he was laughing.

The night Messy Man was killed, I was sitting around with my brothers, my mama, and him in the kitchen. He was joking around and saying, "If y'all hear gunshots, that's going to be me. Y'all better call the police." My mama said, "Boy, you better stop talking like that." She always says a person can feel their death. She told us to go to bed, and he said, "Come on man, I'ma walk y'all in the room." He hung out with us for a few more minutes and then said, "Man, go to sleep. I'ma be here tomorrow." Something in me felt like I might not see him again. Maybe 25 minutes later, I heard gunshots. I heard them repeated in my head hundreds of times. After

Gentilly Fair, courtesy of Lynette Phillips.

the last shot, I closed my eyes tight.

Next day was school. I couldn't pay attention in class, and when I came home, everybody's eyes were red. Kimani walked up to me, crying and talking at the same time. When he finally caught his breath, he said, "Doodie, you remember those gunshots you said you heard last night? It was Messy Man."

I could've just dropped dead. I was in a trance for a long time. I couldn't eat or sleep for days. The day of the funeral I felt so bad all I did was sit in the middle of my room where he used to sleep and stare at the wall. I didn't cry, just remembered all the good times we had with him. He treated us like we were his kids. His death didn't make any sense. There weren't even any rumors about it.

FAVORITES

Kenneth: Where did you learn to fight?

Kimani: My daddy, Kenny Martin. I'd put my hands up and then he'll just swing. He'll tell me which way to move my arms, and then, if he hits me, it's a problem that I'm not holding up my hands right.

Kenneth: And who else?

Kimani: My uncle Irvin Phillips and my brother, Kenneth Phillips—

Kenneth: Yes, I know. We used to fight together sometimes. You know how to fight, but your skill's not like mine. You're not the type to be fighting, though. You used to, like, be friendly and stuff. That wasn't me.

Kimani: If somebody is trying to pick on me that is bigger than me, you're always are around. My other brother is usually busy.

Kenneth: Oh yeah. I don't play all that. How do you think Dad had an influence on you?

Kimani: I learned how to lift weights, and every time I'd do something bad in the elementary, he used to come to the school and try to embarrass me. He stayed on me. If I asked him if I could go outside, he would say, "No, do your homework first."

Kenneth: All right, I'm gonna tell you. Remember that day Dad had a shoot-out, and me and you jumped in that closet and the pole fell on us. Do you remember that?

Kimani: I remember that. And when my daddy was living in New Orleans, he parked by a place and ran up there to go get a drink. There were people out there that were about to have a fight, and then a man pulled out a gun. Me and you were in the back seat right by the action, and you ducked me down and then you got down. The man ran off and my daddy came back. He was sorry for leaving us in the car like that.

Kenneth: Oh, yeah. We were on St. Charles that day and our daddy ran into a daiquiri shop, and all of a sudden some guys just started fighting directly in front of our daddy's car. When I saw that man with the gun, I just pushed you down and ducked over you in the back of the car. If anything happened, I'd rather go before you. Do you think Daddy has favorites between us?

Kimani: [*Shaking his head*]

Kenneth: Like you're his favorite?

Kimani: No, Doodie.

Kenneth: Yeah, he does. Just to let you know. He does.

Finally Heard
Him Say It

My mama taught me how to tie my shoes and how to spell my name. My daddy taught me how to ride my first bike, my times tables, and stayed on me about school. As I grew older, our relationship started to change.

My dad treated my little brother better than me. I was ashamed of that because I was always left out. He took my brothers and me to see my auntie Sheila. I was sitting on the sofas and they were talking about us. I heard my daddy say, "Kimani's gonna be my lil gangsta. He's gonna be a thug and Lil Kenneth's gonna be the lil scared one. He ain't gonna be nothing like his pa." I wanted to say, "I don't want to be like you, and I'm not going to be like you."

My father used to listen to what some people said. When I was about 14, I was on the phone with my dad, and he asked me to call Kimani on three-way at his job—the Touch of Paris, a barbershop near our house—so we could all talk. He asked Kimani to put his boss on the phone. He introduced himself. I knew he was drinking because he was getting emotional. He said, "Take care of my boy, man. But see my other son, Lil Kenneth, I think that nigga gay, man." He said it twice. When I realized what he was saying, I cried because I finally heard him say it. I was like, "Damn, that shit hurt." What kind of man would go to another man that he doesn't know and talk about his own son?

That's when I said, "Fuck you," and threw the phone. My mama was like, "What's wrong, Doo-die?"

"He called me gay."

Kenneth Martin and Kenneth Phillips, courtesy of Irma Phillips.

Kenneth: What was it like to leave for Katrina without me?

Kimani: You were about to come by us until the water got high, and my grandma told you it's too high for him so you went back upstairs. When we left, I just had my mama. Terrance had gone to Houston with his best friend Ahyaro before us. Then, me and mama stayed on the Causeway for so long. We stayed out there for a day and a half. I'd go to sleep, and then I'd let her go to sleep. We'd just watch each other, and all that. I saw helicopters coming down from the sky, taking people out there. I just had my mama— we didn't have no money or nothing. Our step dad had her wallet and her I.D. when he went to Baton Rouge.

Kenneth: He left with us.

Kimani: We didn't have nothing. Yeah, I was worrying about you and my grandma, but I was crying when my dog died. We considered my dog our little brother.

Kenneth: Sir, what did you think when you first saw me in Houston?

Kimani: Well, like my brother had been away. I say it's like you moved away to another country or something. When I first saw you, we almost started crying. I hadn't seen you since the rain started pouring down. Yeah, I hadn't seen you in two months. You had a bush.

Kenneth: I did look different, I ain't gonna lie.

Reunited in Houston

My mama's big sister, Loren, came and got me from Richard, Louisiana. I was staying with my grandma, my great grandma, my two cousins and my aunt. I couldn't wait to get to Houston to see my brothers and my mother. On our way, I fell asleep. My aunt had the radio on, dancing as she drove. By the time I woke, we were there. Everything was so different— everything was so clean. Until I got into the apartments, and then everything went back to how it used to be. The apartments looked like another project. It was just filled with Mexicans. As my aunt pulled into the driveway, everybody stopped and stared. I guess they had never seen us before.

Loren called upstairs and told Kimani to come help me carry my stuff. When I was getting out of the car. I saw a person wearing all red walking towards me. It was Kimani—I'd know his walk from anywhere. I felt tears running down my face while I hugged my brother. It felt so good to see my family again. Then I turned around to see Terrence and my mother. I cried even harder.

While I was staying with my grandmother, I would call my mom and ask when she was coming to get me. She would always say, "I'm coming," but she never came even though she tried her best to find somebody to pick me up.

We decided to go grocery shopping. It was a good feeling to walk and talk to my brothers again, even though Kimani told me some bad news about Mr. Greg, one of my daddy's closest friends. He died during Katrina. The rumor was that he died trying to save someone's life. I couldn't believe it when Kimani told me.

We walked into Walmart with one basket and left with six. It was just me, my brothers, and our mama pushing them all. Terrance kept calling me beady-head because I hadn't had a haircut in so long, and my mama laughed so hard she couldn't breathe.

Going down a bumpy street on the way home, two of the Hawaiian Punches fell off the basket. It was so loud we thought it was somebody shooting. We all jumped and started walking faster. After carrying all that heavy stuff up almost twenty steps, my mama said, "Y'all remember after every time we made groceries, Kobey would always take our sandwich meat and run? We always thought that we left the meat at the store, but then I'd go in the back and there would be meat packs either in the closet or under the bed." We were laughing and saying how much we missed him. And then they asked me, "Man, where were you? We looked all over for you!" I told them me and my cousin Brandon ran half of the bridge looking for them.

It felt weird with all of us sleeping in one room with no beds, just a carpet and six blankets. Before we went to bed, Terrance started cracking jokes.

The next day, Kimani took me out to show me around. We opened the door and the sun was shining right on our porch. He started telling me about Crips and Bloods, and I was like, "What is a Crip and a Blood?" Terrance said the Bloods wear all red and the Crips wear all blue. Kimani said, "They beefing out here—the Crips and the Bloods don't get along."

Kimani, Terrance, and Kenneth at their apartment in Houston, courtesy of Irma Phillips.

I asked, "Which one am I?"

"What you think, fool?"

One of the first things I wanted to do was get my hair cut. My hair grows fast and it's wavy and thick. I had grown a thick bush about two inches long in Richard, but my cousin cut it off. I wasn't happy with the results, but it was better than nothing. Kimani and Terrance told me there was a barbershop in the strip mall nearby.

We walked over, talking about the Astrodome. Terrance said, "Man, you should've been there. They had people cutting hair, they had a gym and everything." I told them the Cajun Dome was a dump. People were walking around in drawers, half naked. Terrance started laughing. I was like, 'Man, what you laughing at?" I looked down and saw a big hole in the back of my shoe. A poor man by the 99 Cent Store asked me if he could have them. I ran home and got a brand new pair of Adidas and ran back to give him the split shoes.

The barbershop wasn't what I was used to. It was filled with Mexican Americans, but I didn't care. I walked to the counter and asked how much they charged. The lady replied, "Three dollars." Kimani started laughing—it seemed so cheap. In the barber's chair, I heard her hit the switch so the clippers could come out. I was nervous, but it came out good, except she didn't give me a lining—the sharp line that frames my face. It felt incomplete and I tapped her on the shoulder and said, "Say, Miss, where is my lining?" She looked at me like she didn't know what I was talking about.

I thought she just didn't care and started to get upset. I had gone to the same person in New Orleans for a long time and I wasn't used to explaining myself. I started to catch an attitude and another barber came up and finished it, but I was still upset because it seemed like she was staring at me. On my way out, I "iffed" her—jumping a little to scare her. It was a failed attempt to gain some control over what was an uncontrollable, confusing time. We returned to the strip mall for candy at the 99 Cent Store and found another barbershop at the very end of the complex. When I looked in the window, I saw an older black woman cutting a man's hair. We peeked in and she asked us if we needed any help. I said, "No, we're just looking," but the place reminded me of New Orleans. Ms. Rhoda cut and braided hair, and soon became our barber.

DON'T WANT TO BE A GANGSTA

Kimani: In Houston, we were staying in apartments. We knew everybody from New Orleans!

Kenneth: I know.

Kimani: Even people from Houston. I didn't want to leave.

Kenneth: But then everybody started leaving, and stuff—

Kimani: Mhm, after we left.

Kenneth: I didn't really like it when we first came back.

Kimani: Because everything was still messed up.

Kenneth: Me and my mom used to watch the news, and they would talk about demolishing the St. Bernard. We were talking like, "No, we don't want it to be done." We should clean up everything with a power washer.

Kimani: I wish the bricks were still there.

Kenneth: But when we went back, everything was moldly, mildew. Roofs caved in. You couldn't live in that type of condition.

Kimani: Yeah, but it always gonna be the B.

Kenneth: Why do you want to be a gangsta?

Kimani: I don't want to be a gangster. Just because

Kenneth and Kimani at Kimani's Eighth Grade graduation, courtesy of the Phillips family.

I rap songs, people think that's a bad influence for me.

Kenneth: That always has been you with that type of stuff. I can't really explain it like I want to. I know what I want to say but I can't put it in words for some reason. You know what I'm talking about.

Kimani: The way I act. Put it like that.

Lynette: The way you dress sometimes.

Kimani: I think it's all right.

Kenneth: And your friends.

Kimani: They ain't friends, man. Go ahead with all that.

Kenneth: Sir, what do you think about when we say you are too nice, like, "You just too nice"?

Kimani: I am nice.

Kenneth: But you're *too* nice. Like how do you feel when we say, "Well Kimani, you too nice"?

Kimani: They could see me as a better person to be doing what I'm doing.

Kenneth: Well, what do you do?

Kimani: Chill. Hang. Take pictures a lot. Rap a lot.

Kenneth: I put it that I'm not friendly.

Kimani: That's how my daddy is. Everybody knows my daddy. I hate to be an enemy to somebody.

Kenneth: I can be nice but, you know, some people just make me mad.

Kimani: I could be asking you what my friends are doing to you, and you're like, "I don't like them dudes you hang with." It ain't like I'm doing something negative with them.

Kenneth: Most of them look like they're up to no good. The only one I can say is cool is Eugene, my mama best friend's son. You two have been best friends for the longest. Half of your friends are in jail.

Kimani: Ain't none of them in jail. Are you talking about dudes from the project? They're not my friends. After Katrina hit, we went separate ways. Whenever we see each other, we just dap and keep walking.

Loretta Sims Martin, by Lindsey Darnell.

III. Interview with My Paternal Grandmother, Loretta Martin

My dad's mom's name is Ms. Loretta S. Martin, but all her grandkids call her Granny. We have special names for each other. I call her G, and she does the same. Growing up, she would always take me places, buy me things, play "pitty pat"—she's got me on "pitty pat." Most kids don't get a chance to have that much fun with their grandma. She's a cool dude.

I've got a hard relationship with my dad, but no one could keep me away from my grandma and my aunts. When I was young, I used to stay with her a lot. She lived in this big blue house on Arts Street in the Eighth Ward. It used to be just me and her. She had a closet filled with clothes everywhere and a box that used to sit on her dresser. I always wondered what was in it. One day I saw her getting dressed for her Eastern Star club's dance, and I heard a lock pop. It was that little box on her dresser. She reached in and pulled out a gold necklace, a gold bracelet, and a few of her gold diamond rings. I tapped her on her leg, and I said, "Granny, why you putting on all that shiny stuff?" She said, "Grandma have to look good when she go out."

Up to this day, as a retired 68 year old woman who worked almost 40 years of her life, she still does the same thing. A long time ago, we went for this super long walk. This walk took forever. We went everywhere. First we went on Bourbon Street then we went to the Riverwalk, then we went to Canal Street, then we caught the bus to St. Claude to go to this big furniture store. I was so tired, I lay on one of the leather sofas. After the long day, she put me in the tub and told me stories.

My granny has a party by her house every single holiday. Our whole family will be there, and I always pay attention to my grandma, smiling to have the whole family together. She taught me almost everything I know about cooking. It runs through the family. She told me if there's nobody I can count on, I can count on her. Some days, I'll call her crying because I feel like I'm in the world alone. I guess as long as my granny has breath in her body, I'll never be alone.

It was just one of those days. We were on the phone and we were talking about all the people that were dying. She said, "Doodie, all I could tell you is live your life like you supposed to and don't let nothing stop you." I said, "I know. I know what type of world I'm living in, I just have to be careful." Everyday I call my grandma to let her know I love her. It's something I must do. If there's anything I lose, it can't be her. Up to this day, we rock the same way and we are going to rock like that until the end.

The interview was at her house on Arts Street in the Eighth Ward. I just like listening to my Granny talk, period. She told me about her marriage at an early age. I can't imagine getting married or having children. She talked to me about my dad, but also told me about our family history. I was really excited to learn I have American Indian heritage. I was running around afterwards telling everybody. Usually people just tell me I look like my dad, but now I can see other features. When I look at myself, I look like a black person, but my hair tells some other stories.

Kenneth: G, where is your family from?

Loretta: My mother was from Grand Isle and most of my daddy's people lived in New York City. His name was Lawrence Sims. His mother was an Indian. She was a beautiful woman. I was small but I remember my grandmother because she had long, pretty hair she used to wear in plats and high cheekbones. My sister knows it good. I never really got to talk to my grandparents.

Kenneth: What neighborhood did you grow up in?

Loretta: I lived lots of places. Sometimes when I'm by myself, I can sit back and think about every house I ever lived in. I've been Uptown, Downtown. When I was a little girl, we were living in a house on Thalia Street—that was before the Melpomene Projects were built, and then we moved to Pilot Land. That's what we called the St. Bernard Projects. During that time, there was a few white people living back there. Mhm. We got along good, though. I never had no problems—black, white, green—cause I tend to my business. And you live a long time tending to your business, honey! If something went on in their house, that's their business. And that's how I was at school, too. I went to Medard H. Nelson. It's still back there. Mhm.

Kenneth: Everybody went there.

Loretta: I was a good student. Most times, when I got in a fight it was when a little boy called himself liking me—I used to beat him up.

Kenneth: Tough. What did you do for fun?

Loretta: I was like a little tomboy. I lived in St. Rose as a little girl when my daddy worked for Illinois Central Railroad. I used to climb trees like little boys.

Kenneth: Me, too.

Loretta: Oh, my daddy had like a little farm there. He raised cows and chickens and all that.

Kenneth: He used to kill them in front you—the chickens?

Loretta: Oh, I used to kill a lot of chickens.

Kenneth: Why?

Loretta: See, we had a big old house on a farm. We lived in one side of the house and my daddy used to keep all his chickens on the other side. That was like our neighbors—them chickens. We used to have a lot visitors and my parents used to talk about we had to go run all the chickens out there and clean that side. You know, hose it out. I said, "Mm, I ain't cleaning. I'ma kill all y'all."

Kenneth: Did you kill all of them?

Loretta: I used to wring their necks. [*Laughs*] Oh Lord. I used to kill them and throw them in the garbage can. It was the little bitty bitties.

Kenneth: Oh, you were killing the babies?!

Loretta: Oh, I wasn't cleaning all that mess. I don't know how many chickens I killed. My daddy whipped me good for that baby—tore me up. If St. Rose could talk, I used to get many whippings. I tell you, it was the good old days. Taught me how to be a woman.

"Men don't act like that."

I've heard that a million times. I hate when people say boys aren't supposed to cry, jump rope, or do hair. We're not supposed to hang around a lot of girls, wear tight clothes or makeup.

One time, I was about to shave my legs because they were getting too hairy and my daddy told me, "No man is supposed to shave his legs." I didn't know.

Men are supposed to be tough. Many talk to each other about football—what team was sad last weekend, or the best. If the Saints are in Chicago, they'll talk about how the Bears can't beat them. On Sunday afternoon, they put on their jerseys and sit down and watch the game, hollering at the screen, "Come on man! Y'all fucking up!" while drinking their beer. A long time ago, some of my dad's friends actually got in a fight because one person's team was beating the other.

I don't like football. I'm tough, but I'm not the type to walk around acting big and bad. I don't listen to much rap like Kimani and Terrance. Kimani loves Soulja Slim's song, "Motha Fuck You" so much, he set it as his ringtone. One time, the principal of his school came over to the house and in the middle of the meeting, his phone started to ring and we all had this look on our face like, "Oh no!" I was surprised the man didn't get up and leave.

My favorite song, on the other hand, is "I Have Nothing" by Whitney Houston. At night, I listen to Mariah Carey, Patty LaBelle, Stephanie Mills, Fantasia, and Kelly Price loud on my headphones so my brothers don't get aggravated. Terrance says, "Kenneth, you listen to the same songs every day!" In my opinion, Mary J. Blige's "Take Me as I Am" is one of the greatest songs ever written. Anybody can get up and sing a song, but she is so strong it sounds like it's reaching out to everybody.

MEN

Loretta: I was 14 when my daddy died. He was 44. He was my world. I was sitting, plaiting his hair. He had one big pompadour and my mama said, "Loretta, come here." They knew he was dead, but I didn't know. They put a mirror in front of him to see if he was still breathing. I said, "Uh uh, I can't leave my daddy right now. What do you want?"

They didn't want to tell me he was dead. He died with a smile. I had a funny feeling in my stomach. The undertaker came and said, "We come for Mr. Sims' body." That's the last thing I know. When they took him off the bed, I blacked out and when I came to, I was in the hospital.

Really, it started off when he picked up the refrigerator. Messed up his back. He couldn't walk and stopped speaking and he just died. But they say he had cancer. We couldn't stay in the projects afterward. My mama's income became too much for the project because of his railroad pension.

I met my husband in the St. Bernard Project right after my daddy died. I lived at 3909 Gibson, Apartment A and his aunt lived at 3909 Gibson, Apartment B. That's how we met. I was a young girl, really young.

Kenneth: How old?

Loretta: Mmm! [*Laughter*]

Kenneth: Twenty-one.

Loretta: No, I married my husband when I was 16.

Kenneth: Oh Lord.

Loretta: Mhmm. Willie Martin—that's my children's daddy—was 18. He was a fine looking man. That was my first boyfriend and my husband because I didn't go out with no boys. That's how I ended up with a baby, because I didn't know about life. He had a large family from Angie, Louisiana, right above Bogalusa. We just got married in Poplarville, Mississippi at the Justice of the Peace with my mama and stepfather, Ernest Jackson. That's who signed my marriage license.

Kenneth: What about his people?

Loretta: We didn't have no big wedding. I didn't want no big wedding—sometimes they don't last. Mine lasted a long time. I had my first son in 1957—altogether we had eight kids; five boys and three girls. Hmm. I had a pretty good life even though I had all those babies. I don't regret none of my kids, though. I love them all, you know. My husband, he took care of what he was supposed to take care of.

I was young. He was young. We are great friends now. He has another wife, which is fine with me. He said I made him get married because I didn't want to take him back. That's the right thing to do. What about the other lady? I don't fault the woman he's with because like I say, "You got to be a willing participant—you got to want to go!" I don't have no bad feelings for her. If we are somewhere together, we hug each other. Ask how each other is doing. I think we were together like 20 years before we separated, and I moved in the Florida Project—me and my kids.

Kenneth: What was it like living in the Florida Project?

Loretta: Before I moved back there, my sister was living back there—Ms. Moss, she was living on Congress Street—and during that time, they had a lot of white people living back there. It was so pretty when the whites were living back there. I hate to say it, but it's true. They had flowers growing, trees. When the black people moved in, the white people moved out. After awhile, there was so much drugs and violence, it drove good people out of there. People were scared.

I lived on Dorgenois Street. Me and my kids. I lost a son in the project. After I lost my son—my second oldest boy—I moved out. Somebody killed him back in 1978. He was trying to stop a fight. That's why—I don't care who's fighting, I don't ever get between anyone. My son lost his life like that. He was 20 years old. He worked for the city. It's just one of those things. I moved from back there.

Kenneth: Where did you meet Grandpa Alfred?

Loretta: In the project.

Kenneth: That's not telling me nothing, Grandma!

Loretta: I met him in the project. He was living with his sister, Brenda. We were pretty close. She sewed—she could make some beautiful clothes. And I used to go visit my sister on Congress Street and play Bid Wis. Four people play—it's just like spades—your grandpa and I were partners. His people lived across the canal in the Lower Ninth Ward. Ms. Irene, his mama, had about 10 children. Might have had more.

Kenneth: I heard Grandpa Alfred used to be a gangster.

Loretta and Alfred dancing, courtesy of Loretta Martin.

Loretta: I don't know nothing about that. He used to live in the St. Bernard Project with his wife, Ethel.

Kenneth: Well, what did he used to do? Good or bad?

Loretta: He was a marvelous painter. He could draw you. Your daddy was the same way.

Kenneth: Oh, yeah.

Loretta: He used sit down and take newspaper and make patterns with it and your aunt Brenda used to make a suit out of that pattern. He never went after his dreams. He was a great artist. He drew a great big eagle right in the bedroom of my house in the Florida Project with two diamonds for eyes. People used to be peeping in my window at night looking at that eagle. Painted my whole house. I had a fabulous house—I really did. And every month, he changed the color of the kitchen. I didn't know nothing about him being a gangsta.

K: You like those bad boys.

Loretta: I was still a Martin when I got pregnant with your daddy, Lil Kenny. We were separated, but I still had his name and so he was legally responsible. My baby was born and he brought me candy and flowers to the hospital. He gave his children money; he gave Kenny money because the law say he was his. Alfred and I were together for about three years.

Kenneth: How old were you when you had my daddy?

Loretta: Mm. I was in my thirties. Because he was born in 74. He was my last baby. All right. What else?

Kenneth: Don't be rushing me.

Loretta: Oh, excuse me.

Kenneth: How was my daddy when growing up?

Loretta: Hmm. Bad.

Kenneth: Like? What did he used to do?

Loretta: A lot of stuff. When Kenny was about seven years old he could actually drive a car. You don't believe that, huh? There was this man living next door in the Florida Project named Mr. Buddy. Ms. Hazer and her husband used to take my son and put him on his lap and taught him how to drive. He actually learned how to drive when he was seven years old. He was a smart little boy. He loved to draw. He can draw anything, just like his daddy.

Kenneth: Mhm. Hmm. How was your relationship with him?

L: I have a good relationship with all my kids. I ain't never had a bad relationship with them because I was their backbone.

Grandpa Alfred Randal

Willie Martin, my grandmother's husband, is my legal grandfather. But my biological grandfather is Alfred Randal, who was my granny's boyfriend for a few years. Even though they didn't stay together, he was close to my daddy. I knew my grandpa used to be gangsta, but I saw the playful side. He read me books before I even knew what a book was. He was there for my first word, my first steps, and I loved him for that.

In 1999, he came to live with my family. He stayed with us for more than four years, and took care of my brothers and me. Every time we saw him, we would run toward him and give him big hugs. He was a good artist and drew all of us. My daddy took after him and drew cards for us. One time, he drew a picture of him and my mama and it looked exactly like them.

Every night before we went to bed, my Grandpa read to us or tried to scare us with these rhymes. "Roses are red, violets are blue. I'm going to sleep, and the monster is under your bed to come and get you."

One early Monday morning, my mom woke us up to go shopping. We came back home and I walked in Papa's room. He was spread out on his bed like he was frozen. He couldn't move, he couldn't talk, all he could was cry. All I could do was cry, too. In the kitchen, I said, "Something is wrong with Grandpa." That's when mom ran in the back and she saw that it was a serious problem and called 911. They rushed him to the hospital and after everything was settled, the doctor told my mother he caught a stroke. The doctor said if he would've laid there a little bit longer, we would've lost him.

My father placed him into the Guste Homes for the elderly where he could be given treatments and taken good care of. One Sunday morning, I called him and asked how he was doing—come to find out he was doing better than I thought. On August 18, 2005, I received a letter from him saying that he loved me and would never forget me. I was wondering what he was talking about.

My Grandma told me after Katrina that he was dead.

COOKING

Kenneth: Where did you work?

Loretta: I worked for Ms. Duball. She was an elderly lady and I cooked and cleaned up for her. I got tired of being a caretaker, so I just went out and got a job cooking. I always did cook because I cooked for my kids. Two of my sons, Willie Martin and Gregory Martin, are chefs. All my children cook. My sister Clotilda worked for a little Greek restaurant for years off Canal Street. She can cook up some Greek food.

Kenneth: How did you learn to cook?

Loretta: My mother was a good cook. When she'd be cooking, I'd be in the kitchen with her trying to see what she was doing—a lot of roasts, cabbage, mashed potatoes, meatballs and spaghetti. I taught myself a lot by being around other cooks, too.

Kenneth: How old were you when you started cooking?

Loretta: I was around 12 years old. When my daddy took sick, I'd be the one who had to cook for the rest of them when I came home from school. My other sisters and brothers, they were grown and working so that made me have to get in the kitchen.

My first job was a breakfast place on Canal and Rampart. From there, I found a job as a chef at the Holiday Inn on Royal Street. We did the cooking for parties and balls. I worked there for 20 years. The hotel closed their restaurant, which was on the tenth floor. A lot of people there took severance pay, but I didn't, because they moved me to another hotel.

I started working at the Crowne Plaza and the Cha-

Both pages: Loretta at work, courtesy of the Loretta Martin.

teau Lemoyne and stayed until 2005 when the hurricane came. Then I retired, but the rent is so high here. I pay 1,100 dollars to live here. And you have your lights and other necessities like cable. I've worked all my life. I worked as a young girl, and I can't get food stamps. The system is messed up.

Kenneth: What's your favorite dish to cook?

Loretta: Aww, gumbo.

Kenneth: Ohh, my favorite!

L: Most times I cook seafood cause my grandbabies like seafood gumbo. I put crabs, shrimps, smoked sausage, crawfish, hot sausage.

Kenneth: Gizzards.

Loretta: You put the gizzards in there. Cut them up. You put a little turkey necks; cut them all up. I could pat myself on the back with gumbo. I make some gumbo! My favorite roast is the crown roast. You buy your pork chops, take the two halves, cut the bones, and sew them together. You fix it like a

crown on your head. Then you put thyme and take a piece of paper, cut it on the ends for decoration, and set it on top. In the middle of it you put seafood dressing—crawfish, crab meat, shrimps. I'm gonna show you how to make that one day.

Kenneth: What about that pepper stuff that you used to make?

Loretta: Oh, stuffed pepper. Some people put rice and ground meat. I don't like that. I don't like rice in peppers. Doesn't look good to me. I make it with shrimp, crabmeat, and cut up the ham.

Recipe for Stuffed Peppers

I've been cooking this recipe for 47 years.

Prepare the ingredients:
2 onions, diced small
1 bell pepper, dice it
2 bunches of green onions (I season mine well)
½ cup fresh parsley
Salt and pepper
About half a pound of ground beef
Half a pound of seasoned ham
About a pound of shrimp, chopped into smallish pieces
One can (8 oz.) of blue claw crab meat

Sauté:
All the seasoning until the onions brown.
Add ground meat, let it cook a little, and follow with the shrimp, crab and ham.
Saute down. Take it off the stove. Let it cool.

Bust six eggs:
Beat them.
Put that in the pan.
Add Italian bread crumbs.
Mix it all together, by hand.

While stuffing is cooling down:
Take 4 bell peppers, cut them in half, and clean out seeds.
Pinch of salt, pepper, and cayenne.

Stuff the peppers by hand:
Sprinkle a little bread crumbs on top.
Put them in oven at 350 degrees with a little water in the pan and cover.
Let them go for half an hour to an hour.

Both pages: Grandma Loretta's social and pleasure clubs, courtesy of Loretta Martin.

WHEN YOU LOSE ONE YOU GET ANOTHER ONE

Kenneth: What do you remember most about your mother?

Loretta: I remember everything about my mother. My mama was an Eastern Star. I was an Eastern Star, too—the Eastern Star of King George. That's a Christian organization. You see these people dressing up with these white uniforms and different color hats on their heads? That's an Eastern Star.

Kenneth: So you were an Eastern Star?

Loretta: I was 42 years old. It's just like the Masons. You ever heard of the Masons? I was the Queen Best Order of the Eastern Star, state of Louisiana. You have to know different things to get into this.

Kenneth: Like what?

Loretta: I can't tell you that.

Kenneth: Don't lie to me. Why can't I know?

Loretta: Cause I can't tell you that.

Kenneth: Oh, it's a secret that y'all have to keep?

Loretta: It's a secret—you had to join to know this. It is something that I can't explain to you.

Loretta: My mama died in my house. I think you were born.

Kenneth: They told me on the day. June the fourth.

Loretta: My mother woke up at four in the morning and said she had to go to the bathroom. She sat on the side of the bed, and said, "Just let mama sit there for a few minutes." She called me Lalechter. "Lalechter, don't rush your mama." I said, "I'm not tryin to rush you, Mama. Take your time. While you in the bathroom, I'm gonna give you a bath and put you another nightgown on so I won't have to disturb you if you go back to sleep before I have to go to work."

My mama was a big old woman. She weighed about 250 pounds. I put her in the tub. But mama was dying then, and I didn't know it. My son picked her up, put her on the bed, and we dressed her. When I called 911, they told me she just died of natural causes.

That was the worst moment of my life. To me, I'd lost everything. I had already lost my daddy. I was trying to buy the house, but I couldn't cope. I had this rocking chair I bought for her to sit in, and she used to just rock in that chair. When I came home in the evening time after we had put my mother away, I saw that chair rocking. I couldn't cope with that. I had to leave there. I told the man I didn't want the house anymore so he sold it to somebody else.

But my mama was passing and there's a little boy. They say when you lose one, you get another one. You're spoiled now—you're a spoiled brat! You're a good kid, though. But you're mean like your daddy. Just like your daddy. I said, "Boy, when that baby was born, you cursed that baby cause he just like you." A spitting image of your daddy. I try not to get in between y'all.

Kenneth: Why do you think I have such a hard time connecting with my daddy?

Loretta: Because y'all are alike. You're just like him, and your ways are so much alike, it's hard to communicate. Y'all can't get along. But you'll be a man after awhile, and you'll understand. It will take you to have a child for you to understand.

Kenneth: I don't want children.

Loretta: Well, I'm just saying. Sometimes children are good for your nerves, baby.

Kenneth: I want a puppy.

Loretta: Boy! Ask the next question.

Kenneth: Almost everything I learned, I learned from you. What was it like helping to raise me?

Loretta: It was beautiful to help raise you. I don't care what happened, you're gonna tell me. I get along with you like you're my son instead of my grandson. I don't have bad grandchildren, but you're like my favorite grandbaby. I was glad I was there for you and I'll be there until God takes you. No matter what the situation is, you can always come to Grandma.

You make your choice and stick to your choice. Don't care what people say about you because they talked about Jesus Christ. And if they talked about that man, you know that they'll talk about me and you. Don't worry about what people say about you. Put that to the side and say, "Oh well. Let them say what they want to say."

I'm My Own Person

Like usual, I was hanging out with Keith, and it was one of those days my daddy was coming for a visit. I ran upstairs for a frozen cup and Keith waited for me downstairs. When I made it back, I saw my daddy, and he told me, "Come here."

I told Keith I'd be back. He said, "What you doing with him?"

"Who, Keith? That's my friend."

He said, "I don't want you with him."

"Why not? All this time we've been friends and you are just telling me this?"

The next day I told my mama what he said, and she reassured me, "How can he tell you who you can or can't be with? Keith is your friend. Can't nobody end that relationship but y'all." Kimani went downstairs and told Keith what my daddy had said. I told Keith, "My daddy could've told me that a million times— that doesn't mean I am going to listen."

Later that day Keith, Willie, and I were walking through the court. Keith said, "You know Kenneth's daddy doesn't like me."

I said, "What makes you say that?"

"Because he doesn't. I can tell by the way he looks at me."

"That doesn't mean nothing. He can't pick my friends. I'm my own person. Man, I don't care."

Willie said to Keith, "You shouldn't care. While we've been friends, I heard people say a lot of things about you, but I don't care."

I told Keith, "I feel the same way."

Keith wiped the sweat off of his face. Willie closed it out talking about my dad, "Yeah, now get out of our business, old bald head ass!" We started laughing. Everybody was looking like, "What are they laughing at?"

It was hot outside when we made it back to our side of the project. We went to sit on my bottom porch and waited until it was time to go inside. Willie asked Keith, "How do you feel when people say you're a fag?"

Keith said, "I really don't give a fuck about what anybody has to say. Keith is going to be Keith. If you don't like it, oh well."

He paused and then said, "Willie."

Willie said, "What?" He said, "How do you feel when people talk about that triangle-shaped bush on your head?"

I was weak, laughing. I'm not trying to play my lil dawg, but his bush was shaped like a triangle. Just to think, we were the only ones outside that night, sitting on the porch, doing nothing with our lives. That's how we used to roll.

Both Pages: Keith Elpaige, by Kenneth Philips.

Kenneth and Keith, by Lindsey Darnell.

LAST DAYS

Kenneth: What do you do for fun now?

Loretta: Look at that television.

Kenneth: That's what I said.

Loretta: I don't go nowhere but that television. I like to watch *Murder She Wrote* with Angela Lansbury. Now, I love the game shows. I love Chuck Norris in anything he plays in. And what's that man's name?

Kenneth: Who?

Loretta: Oh, I was crazy about him. With the ponytail?

Kenneth: Steven Segal?

Loretta: Oh, that's a fine man. [*Laughter*]

Kenneth: Eww!

Loretta: He is! Don't cover your ears. I bought all his tapes cause I like to watch him. And the church is so far away from here without transportation. They are building a church right there, but I'm gonna be going away from here when it's finished.

Kenneth: Where you going?

Loretta: I'm going back to Ft. Worth.

Kenneth: No, you're not. You're not gonna leave me down here, Grandma.

Loretta: You don't want me leaving you, period. It's so hard down here, honey. I was raised and born here. It's just since Katrina things are so rough. People barely can make it, and I barely can make it myself. I thank God for what I have—my health, my strength. So it wakes me up in the morning. That's beautiful. So many people have gone. So I thank God for that.

We're living in the last days. Katrina was a wake up call to all of us because we waded through water, getting to the Superdome. We walked in water and carried grandchildren. They had to carry those kids on top of their heads because the water was up to here on us. That's why me being so short, the water was on me worse.

I lived in Ft. Worth. The people were nice and I had a nice house, two porches—front porch and a back porch. I was paying 570 dollars a month for that house. You think you can get that here? Uh uh. You're not gonna get it here. 1,100 dollars for two-bedrooms. But I'm used to working. I'm not used to living on the retirement. I'm used to going to work and living for the paycheck. If you sit down too long your body gets stiff. So I gotta get myself active again, and when I do that, look out. I'll be ready.

Irma Phillips, by Lindsey Darnell.

IV. Interview with My Maternal Grandmother, Irma Phillips

My grandma Irma Phillips has yellowish skin with freckles and blond hair. She wears prescription shades and a cross around her neck. In the St. Bernard, she stayed right across the street from us. She wasn't an outside person, but whenever you needed her, she was there. Every time I went to visit, she greeted me by saying, "Hey, K.K.," and I always left with peppermints, cranberry juice, and strawberry banana yogurt.

My grandma kept us close to God. It was a wonderful thing to teach us. She gave us all kinds of Bible stories like *Behold the Lamb* and *Jesus Walks*, and lots of coloring books with pictures of Adam and Eve. Our weekends were full of church. On Saturday nights, she took us to Bible Study and on Sundays we went to church services at the Beacon Light Baptist Church, one of the biggest churches in the city. Every bench was filled with people. They advertised the church on billboards around the city. My grandma had been going there before I was even born.

Church was her sanctuary and we had to be on time. Kimani, Terrance, and I walked over to her apartment in clean, presentable clothes. She was usually dressed in a blouse, slacks, and baby doll shoes. Her good friend, Mr. Youngblood, picked us up and drove us. We were often the first ones there. We beat the pastor, the choir, and the ushers. The camera lady, who filmed the service so that people in the back could see, wasn't even there. The church services were long—two or three hours—and my grandma sat there and took notes the whole time.

She raised three children on her own: Loren, Irvin, and my mother Lynette. She helped our mother take care of us since we came home from the hospital and went back and forth to help our great-grandmother.

She worked at Bynum's, a black-owned pharmacy near the St. Bernard, for many years and cared about our education. When I was younger she'd ask me what I wanted to be when I grew up, and I'd reply, "A Ninja Turtle."

When my grandma came back to New Orleans after Katrina, she stayed in a FEMA trailer at her sister's house on Dreux Street to help take care of their mama. Now she lives on the second floor of a fourplex down the street. She likes it because of the spiral staircase.

I was so used to seeing her every day in the St. Bernard. Now we might see her every other week. This interview gave me a chance to catch up with her. Going around and around, up the steps to her apartment, I was thinking I'd learn a lot about our family's history. She told me some things I didn't know, like our family used to speak Creole French and lived in New Orleans and LaPlace for a long time. I've never been to LaPlace, where her dad's family is from, but now I'm interested in visiting and traveling to get to know more parts of my history.

Kenneth: Where did you grow up?

Irma: Here in New Orleans, Louisiana. We lived around the Eighth Ward on Mandeville Street. Then we moved to Industry Street for awhile and then moved into the Desire Public Housing Development. We were around for Hurricane Betsy. I was 13. Being that young, it wasn't like, "Oh, something bad," during the storm. The next day with the water and so forth, that was serious. Bodies floating—snakes and rats. Some friends and neighbors drowned.

But we only had flood water for less than a week and that was it. We never had to leave town. We survived, stayed right there. We should have learned from 1965 with Betsy, compared with Katrina in 2005. It's just sad. We should have been well-protected.

Kenneth: Where are your parents from?

Irma: My parents were from New Orleans. On my mom's side, my grandmother, Rosaleen Miles, was from the city, but my grandfather, Joesph Miles, and his sisters—my great aunts—were from LaPlace, Louisiana. We used to call his sister Lucinda "Nannan Siseen." Don't ask me what that means. I didn't really understand the Creole French. When I was a little girl, we visited Nannan Sisseen almost every weekend. She was right across the street from where they used to wash vegetables. The tracks separated her house from the little market place.

Kenneth: What were your parents like?

Irma: I wasn't close to my father. My mom, I was very close to her and my grandparents who practically raised me while my mom was holding down two jobs doing hotel and hospital work.

Irma (in pigtails) with her grandmother Rosaleen, courtesy of Loren Phillips.

Before going home from school, we would stop by my grandparents' house right on the side of the Galvez overpass to have graham crackers and milk with Bosco in it. My grandmother told me she stopped going to school in third grade, but she taught me my math, multiplications and everything.

Kenneth: Did you go to church as a child?

Irma: Yes, on Sunday we attended Second Morning Star Baptist Church three times that day. It was located on South White Street. In the morning, we would have Bible study. Go back in the afternoon, they would get together singing, and the preacher was preaching. The late service was similar to the afternoon.

My grandmother taught me how to interpret dreams. Yes. She went from the Bible really, because when you read the Bible, it's visions and dreams. When you're sleeping, God will come to you in your sleep and talk to you.

Church

Every week, my grandma Irma got us all together for church—Terrance, Kimani, me, and sometimes Brandon. Terrance and I would sit together on one side, and she would separate Kimani, putting him on the other side of her.

We joined Beacon Light Baptist Church in 2002 and we were all baptized there. Beacon Light is one of the biggest churches in the city, more than seven hundred people a week, and television screens all over broadcasting the service as it happens.

My first day there, I didn't think church could be that fun. We were singing songs, praying, and listening to the Word of God. Kimani's and my favorite song was *We Lift Our Hands*:

We lift our hands in the sanctuary
We lift our hands to give you the glory
We lift our hands to give our praise
And we will praise you for the rest of our days.

Before going to church Kimani always asked Grandma, "Are they going to sing my song at church today?"

"I don't know Mani, we will have to see when we get there."

During the singing and praying the pastor would speak on the Word, and the elders lifted their hands in the air, and Kimani and I started rocking along with them. Every once in awhile, he'd throw his hands up like the police were telling him to freeze, and I'd bust out laughing.

I was 11 years old when my Grandma told me, Terrance, Kimani, and Brandon that we were going to be baptized. I was a little nervous.

Kimani and I dressed alike, as usual, and when we got to the church, they put us in white pants, a button-down shirt, and an all-white head wrap. We sat in the front of the church, and during the service, they asked us to stand—about 30 of us—and go to the second floor. Everyone clapped as we walked past. I walked past my mom, and she was smiling at me.

We got on the elevator, all these people of different ages dressed in white, and I was getting too nervous. We walked down a long hallway and there was a preacher standing in the water with a camera pointed toward him. They were broadcasting us being baptized back to the main sanctuary. When I got near the front, I kept letting people go in front of me. I was so scared I had chill bumps.

Then it was my turn. I put my foot on the first step and started to shake. The pastor grabbed my hand and helped me walk into the water, and kneel. He said a short prayer, put his hand on my forehead, and pushed me back into the cold water. The chill bumps got worse as I climbed the stairs out of the tub.

I hugged Kimani, and then we went back to the changing room to dry off and change our clothes. We walked back into the front of the sanctuary to a standing ovation. The service ended and we went to be with our families.

I was proud of myself for being baptized, for turning my life over to Jesus. I had always pictured myself living in the project and fighting for the rest of my days. My mom always says trust and believe and He'll work it out for you, and I believe that.

SHE WOULD TALK ABOUT THE LOVE

Kenneth: What are some things that you did for fun as a child?

Irma: We used to sit down with my grandparents and listen to their stories of them when they were growing up. When my grandmother's mom died, her father had to raise five of them by himself. It was hard but they made it, and it was so much love and that's all she would talk about is the love.

Kenneth: Could you tell me some of the bad things that happened in your life?

Irma: As what? An adult or a child?

Kenneth: Either one.

Irma: Oh, as a child, my grandfather whipped my butt for being hard-headed.

Kenneth: But you were a good child.

Irma: That particular time, I didn't listen. My grandfather was saying his prayers one morning and my grandmother was in the kitchen cooking. She said, "Whatever you do, little Irma, don't go in the room by the other kids cause your grandfather is saying his prayers." When my grandfather finished saying his prayers, it was on. So we all wound up with a beating with a cat of nine tails—a stick with nine different whips on it so when they hit you, that one time, that's really like nine licks. And it hurts. Big time.

Kenneth: Could you tell me some of the best things that ever happened in your life?

Irma: Traveling with my grandparents to Pensacola, Florida, Chicago, LaPlace. Just being with them.

Traveling Wasn't My Thing

Before Katrina, I didn't really care for any place other than the St. Bernard. Every time my mom would make us go somewhere, I would get mad because I thought it was boring.

Like most of the children from the project, I walked to Medard H. Nelson Elementary every day. From home to school and back was my main route. Detours included Charity Hospital, grocery shopping at Winn Dixie, and the Beacon Light Baptist Church. Once, I went to my daddy's job at Dickie Brennan's Steakhouse with Kimani. My daddy, taking after all the cooks in his family, was the kitchen manager over ten chefs. We sat at the bar, and the bartender looked out for us while we ate steak and fries, shrimp, and chocolate cake. He poured us Cokes and we pretended we were drunk, swaying back and forth. Kimani took it a little too far and slammed his head into the bar like Homer Simpson.

On Saturdays, we made an occasional trip to Canal Street, the heart of the city and the dividing line between Uptown and Downtown. It's full of big buildings, hip-hop clothing stores, and shoe stores like Foot Locker and The Athlete's Foot.

I used to love going because sometimes we saw friends from school. Canal was full of everybody—white, black, Vietnamese. I wondered, "Where do all these people come from?" I always thought the project was made for black people and I didn't know too much about other neighborhoods. I've learned since that I was right. The St. Bernard was created by the Housing Authority of New Orleans as a segregated black project. That's why there was only one white lady living there.

Katrina really got my traveling train started. I had never traveled outside the city, and within a few years I had been to Lafayette and Richard, Louisiana, with my grandma. I lived in Houston and went to Memphis, the beaches in Alabama, and to Florida to see my dad. Being in these new places with new people, I began to picture myself living other places—Barcelona, London, Honduras, somewhere in West Africa. I'd go anywhere.

I didn't miss traveling until I started. I was comfortable where I was, but now I want to keep traveling. I think I could have another home in the world.

CHILDREN

Kenneth: When did you decide that you wanted to have children?

Irma: After I got married. My husband and I decided we'd have three or four children, but I only had three. And that was it.

Kenneth: What was it like to be a single mom?

Irma: After my divorce, it was hard, but I made it through the grace of God. It was a struggle, but I made sure that my kids had. I did without many times, but I made sure they had because I love them.

Kenneth: When did you realize you would have to do it on your own?

Irma: After my husband left out the door.

Kenneth: What did you have to give up?

Irma: Some of the fun. What I did, it was a lot.

Kenneth: What was my mom like when she was a child?

Irma: [*Laughter*] Your mom, she was hard-headed at times. Remember the story? She was supposed to go to a party around the corner from the house, but wound up way on St. Bernard and Claiborne Avenue. They had a drive-by shooting that night, and she was one of the victims. She was shot in the foot and was on crutches for about a month. She always tells y'all, "Don't be hard-headed and don't lie to your parents."

Kenneth: Who was the problem child?

Irma: Irvin. The reason why he was like that, his daddy promised to be there for him, and he wasn't. It just really hurt him and made it hard for him to deal with other issues.

Kenneth: When did you move to the St. Bernard?

Irma: I think it was June of 1976. My oldest sister was living in the development at the time and I wanted to be near her. The Lord answered my prayer and we moved in.

Kenneth: In that same apartment that you lived in when we were there?

Irma: Yes. You know, when I was visiting my sister, this particular apartment, 1500 Milton, Apartment D, always captured my eyes. And that's the apartment, thank you Lord, that I was blessed to move into.

I was born with a veil. And a lot of people don't understand what a veil is. I was told by my grandmother and my mom that it's a thin piece of skin, which covers the face of the baby if a woman's water doesn't break when she is in labor. They used to take and sell it to the seamen. And the seamen would be able to tell whether a storm was coming. A lot of times, I can see things before they actually happen. It was scary at first because I saw things no one else was seeing. Sounds ridiculous, but it's a gift.

Kenneth: When my uncle died—

Irma: Who, Irvin?

Kenneth: Yeah. This was my dream: I was in the back of the court and he was walking towards the store and I called his name. He went to waving slow. I went to running, but it was like I was in slow motion.

Irma: Running is death.

Kenneth: So I'm running and everything went black for a minute and I woke up. Then that day almost the same thing happened, but it was Terrance calling his name. It wasn't me. And I was looking at him, but he just disappeared.

Irma: Yeah, it's just like his soul was gone. It's just the shell that has to go and rest. But just like grandmother used to always call it, your soul leaves the body before anything really happens. Timing is very important to God. Before you're even born, the place and the time is already set for your death. Death walks with us every day. And you go to church, study the Bible and you learn a lot. It prepares you—get to know God and let him fight your battles.

They said the children were playing basketball in the court, right in the same area where they killed Irvin. He passed by and wasn't saying anything. And a few minutes later, they heard the shot.

Dreams & Visions

Terrance, my grandmother Irma, and I always talk about and interpret our dreams. My grandma also knows about visions, explaining that, "God's revelation to the prophets were usually by visions and come to you when you are awake."

When I was in third grade, I dreamt about my cousin Brandon running through a field. In the dream, I was like a camera—not really there. Brandon was running through the tall grass, and suddenly he was shot. In the dream, I could see his blood, and him laying on the ground.

Not long after, Brandon's father, Uncle Irv, was shot, running from the bullets. I always believed in my grandma's interpretations, but after that I knew it was true.

One time, we were coming from church, riding home with my grandma's friend. We were cruising toward our house, on Gibson. My grandma said, "I have a feeling something is going to happen in this driveway." I felt it too, and I agreed, as did Terrance. The next night, Marshall was killed in the driveway.

Now when I have a dream, or Terrance does, I call my grandma. The last one Terrance had, he was running from someone trying to kill him and he ran all the way to my grandma's house. It took her a while to answer, because she was on the phone. When he got her attention, he said, "Grandma, someone is trying to kill me," and she said, "Who, him?" and Terrance turned around, and someone shot him.

When he called her and told her the dream, she told him that things are often the opposite of what they seem. Blood, for instance, can mean victory.

One night I went to sleep before everybody, and I had a dream. I was asleep, and it felt like I woke up, and was sitting up in my bed. This shadow kept walking past the door to my room, and it sounded like my uncle Irvin calling my name.

I stood up to go to the door, but as I started, I woke up.

I called my grandma, and she told me that it was a good thing that I didn't get to the door, because that is how it is when death is knocking at your door.

After so many calls to my grandma for dream interpretations, I can now interpret my own dreams, and most of the time, they come true.

Irvin **"DJ Irv"** Phillips

April 4, 1968 - February 26, 2001 - Eternal Life

Opening Prayer	Rev. London

Reading of the Obituary

Musical Selection

Scripture Reading	Timothy Lewis

Words of Comfort

"A Legend In His Time"	Mia X
Reflections	Lorèn K. Phillips
Closing Prayer/Benediction	Rev. London

And I saw a new heaven and a new earth: for the first heaven and the first earth were passed away; and there was no more sea.

And I John saw the holy city, new Jerusalem, coming down from God out of heaven, prepared as a bride adorned for her husband.

And I heard a great voice out of heaven saying, Behold, the tabernacle of God is with men, and He will dwell with them, and they shall be His people, and God himself shall be with them, and be their God.

And God shall wipe away all tears from their eyes; and there shall be no more death, neither sorrow, nor crying, neither shall there be any more pain: for the former things are passed away.

　　　-Revelations 21:1-4

Irvin "DJ Irv" Phillips, born April 4, 1968, in New Orleans, Louisiana, at his Father's request ascended to the feet of our Lord and Savior. Irvin is and shall remain the loving son of Ms. Irma James Phillips, devoted brother of Lorèn K. Phillips and Lynette M. Phillips. Irvin was the proud father of Brandon, Irvin and Travis, uncle of Terrance, Kenneth and Kimani. Great-Grandson of the late Joseph and Roseline Miles, grandson of Ms. Irma James, Nephew of Clarissa, Robert, Sadie, Olive, Howles, Frederick, Moses, Caroline and Frank, companion of Deon and cousin, friend and brother to many others.

Entertainment Accomplishments: Co-founder of 'Bounce' music, "Wha Dey At?", "Woke 1 Mornin'" (singles), DJ Irv's Mega Mix 2001, the motivating vehicle behind Da R.U.D.E Magazine, recognized as one of the South's most accomplished Club DJ's and one of the innovators of club scratching in the '80's.

"As the rumor mill turns, the Word of God shall be our strength. We'd like to extend our gratitude for the words of comfort, your visits, phone calls and cards." *-The Phillips Family*

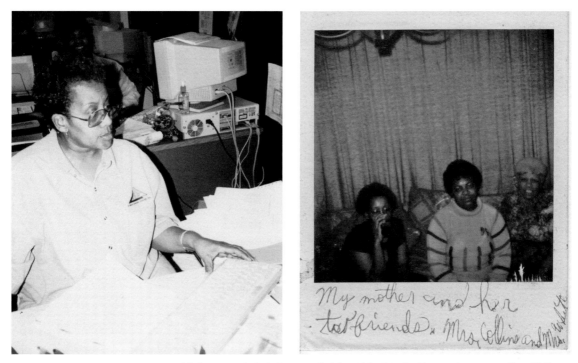

Left: Irma at work. *Right:* Irma , on the left, with her friends,. Photographs courtesy of Irma Phillips.

WHERE YOU'VE BEEN

Kenneth: How did you feel about raising your kids in the St. Bernard?

Irma: I was happy. The St. Bernard was very helpful and pleasant for us. I know a lot of people who lived in the St. Bernard and other developments who were hard working people. Some became doctors, nurses, entrepreneurs, lawyers, and politicians. It's not where you live, it's what you want out of life—your dreams and your goals.

Kenneth: What kind of job did you have to help support your children?

Irma: I was a doctor's assistant in a clinic across the street from the St. Bernard and a medical biller at a hospital.

Kenneth: How did you meet Ms. Vivian?

Irma: Ms. Vivian. When I first moved in the St. Bernard housing development, she lived in the apartment on the first floor, and I was on the second floor. She was really not only a friend but like a sister to me. She had my back and I had her back as they would say. She's a very good friend. Ms. Vivian was something like a Madea. They used to call her "Mom-mie." Very kind, honest, reliable. Very sweet. She used to watch your mom, Uncle Irvin and Loren while I worked and took care of my business and I watched her children.

67

Kenneth: How did we get to Richard, Louisiana after Hurricane Katrina?

Irma: After we were rescued from New Orleans, they drove us to Lafayette, Louisiana, where we had to stay in the Cajun Dome for a couple days. There was a pastor from a church in Lafayette, and they took us to Richard and let us stay at the Acadian Baptist Church's resort out there. They let us stay out there for a month. They treated us like kings and queens.

Kenneth: It was. We had to serve the food.

Irma: Yeah, you had to help out, too. And everything was a red carpet for us. We were homesick, but you do what you have to do. We survived, and I thank God for that. You knew where you'd been but you didn't know where you're going. That's the thing. We were homeless.

Kenneth: I wasn't homeless, but—

Irma: No? You were homeless when they rescued us from St. Bernard, and we had to stay on 610 for hours. You were homeless.

Kenneth: I wasn't homeless. I had a box and an MRE.

The Acadian Baptist Church's resort in Richard, Louisiana, by Irma Phillips.

Irma: Yeah, the army fed us on the bridge. But just watching the people, and then that water...We didn't know whether my mom and my sisters were still alive—I didn't know whether they drowned. We didn't have a way to get in touch with anyone to find out what was going on.

68

Time Cover

Come to find out, my great grandma and great auntie Saddie were evacuated to Tennessee. They came back to Louisiana to stay with us in Richard.

One afternoon, my aunt Olive and cousin Lathan decided to take a ride to Walmart while my grandma, my other cousin La'Chanae (aka Lala), and I stayed with my great-grandmother. On their way out the door, my great-grandma reminded my aunt to not forget her Italian dressing.

I went in the room to see if my grandma needed anything. I heard my cousin LaLa scream my name, "K.K.!" I ran because I thought it was important.

I said, "What's wrong?" She said, "Could you fix me some cereal?" Then she started laughing and said, "Sit down, let's watch a movie." We started watching "Madea's Family Reunion."

When my aunt and cousin came back, Lathan ran in saying, "Look what we found!" It was *Time* magazine with my great aunt Saddie pushing my great grandma through almost four feet of water. My aunt was screaming for help while my great grandma just held on as tight as she could to the wheel chair.

I was shocked. My mouth stood open for a couple of minutes. My grandma started to cry, and she gave her mother a hug. Maybe millions of people saw this picture and thought it really was an American tragedy. For my family, the separation during the evacuation was hard, but the bigger tragedies came before and after the storm. Messy Man. Uncle Irvin. Kobey. We lost them for good.

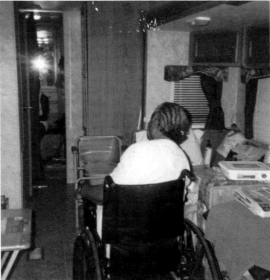

Top: Aunt Olive Daw and her daughter La'Chanae picked up Kenneth, Terrance, and Kimani in New Orleans after they came back from Houston and drove to Baker, Louisiana, to surprise Irma and her mom, who were living in a FEMA trailer in Renaissance Village. *Bottom:* Irma James, Kenneth's great-grandmother in the trailer. Photographs by Irma Phillips.

Both images: Renaissance Village, the Federal Emergency Management Agency (FEMA) trailer park, by Irma Phillips.

The St. Bernard Housing Development closed after Katrina, by Kenneth (*left*) and Irma Phillips (*middle and right*).

SEASONS

Kenneth: What did you think about the St. Bernard being torn down?

Irma: I was angry at first because the Housing Authority of New Orleans and the Department of Housing and Urban Development (HUD) could have kept the buildings. Those old buildings were very sturdy and strong. They've been through all the storms you can name. The bricks have survived. I even mailed letters to HUD and suggested that they tear the old part of the development down, but take the new part of the development and just remodel the inside for historic purposes. Everything is the cheap way out. If you sneeze, your neighbor can hear you. It's true. I like something that's strong and you feel secure. They never responded to any of the letters. We have to move on. We have no control over it.

Kenneth: Where do you go to church now?

Irma: Fellowship Missionary Baptist Church on Prytania. It's like this: The shepherd knows his sheep. I decided I didn't want a big old church where the pastor only knows the people who are giving big money. He knows all members.

Kenneth: What do you like to do during your free time?

Irma: As a child I wrote poems. I was going to do a book about Irvin, but each time I tried it was too much hurt so I stopped. Now it's a love novel, and it's about men being hard-headed.

I listen to music, gospel and sometimes R&B. I'm still alive. [*Laughter*] I love *Psalms*. "Psalm 23," the

Lord Is My Shepherd. "110," Your enemies become your footstool. "37," "35." And I read about Job.

Our life is divided. There are seasons. You have a good season, a bad season, a crying season, a grieving season. He's going to get all the glory, but you have to endure the trials and tribulations. Only the strong survive. There's just some things I'm trying to deal with now, like with my child and so forth.

I've learned obedience. Just listening to our pastor and learning about the Lord makes me happy. God does not close a door without opening another. I don't want to block my blessings by being disobedient.

Kenneth: Do you worry about us?

Irma: I do. I love you all so much and I'm used to living so close to you. Things happen so fast. What happened to Irvin, it just really puts me on alert. I pray for all of you every day—I pray for everyone, but special prayers for y'all, that the Lord keeps you all safe and will be a hedge around you. I know your mother does the best she's able to do. My grandmother used to worry about us, too, to make sure we had everything we needed and so forth. It's just that love and being so close. Yeah.

Loren Phillips, courtesy of Loren Phillips.

V. Interview with My Aunt, Loren Phillips

I never really have a chance to hang out with Loren. Maybe some days she'll pass by my grandma and I'll be over there and she'll ask me about school. One time she asked me to go grocery shopping with her. The women on my mom's side of the family always use this same trick. They'll ask you to go to the store and say, "I'm not going to be long." Loren used that trick on me. We went shopping at Save-A-Lot. We were in there at least an hour. She couldn't find what we were looking for, but I never complain when I'm with my aunt because she's always good to me.

I've always looked at my aunt as this gorgeous woman. When I was young, I thought she was Latina because she has long black curly hair and bright skin.

She loves to sing and listens to Lady GaGa. One time she gave me this pimp-looking hat, but I lost it during Katrina. It was all black with a feather on the side and I liked it.

I would compare myself to Loren as far as education goes. We both love to read, write, and we both like good conversation. She is a writer, producer, and manager in New Orleans. She published a magazine for years called *Da R.U.D.E.* on hip hop in New Orleans. She lives in Houston now but came in for my grandma's birthday. I learned a lot about our family history from both of them.

Kenneth: Who did you look up to when you were growing up?

Loren: My mother, and my great-grandmother, Rosaleen Miles. I spent every Sunday with my great grandmother at her house on 1812 Clouet Street. The area she lived in was a very diverse neighborhood. The lady who lived across the street from her was white. Most of the people who had worked most of their lives purchased the houses and retired. She was very docile, very calm, very, very quiet and very helpful.

Irma: Humble.

Loren: She taught me the Lord's Prayer. Until the time she was in her nineties, every time she said her prayers at night, she got on her knees. She had this thing, you have to humble yourself before God. You don't say your prayers in your bed; you bow before Him and pray.

She was of Native American, French, Anglo-Saxon, and Haitian heritage. She had these extremely high cheekbones and long hair down her back, and she was real petite. She was real pretty—real, real pretty. I used to watch her on Sundays when she dressed for church. It was very couture, very European. There were never the decorated hats like today's church lady.

I thought, "I want to be like her." She reminds you of someone from an old classical movie. It's like watching one of those old Bette Davis movies, when you see the ladies put the hats on and the gloves and the jackets. And she would brush her hair back, twist it into a real bun, and then she put her hat on. Sometimes they were little bitty hats with the felt and the

Roseline and Joseph Miles, courtesy of Loren Phillips.

velvet that she'd put on one side. And then she'd put her gloves on.

I have a picture of my grandmother, her sister, and her sister's husband in a juke joint. Even to go to the juke joint, they were in dresses and heels and sitting at these tables, having cocktails. And the heels looked like Christian Lacroix shoes that would be 800 dollars now. They would wear these shoes every day.

My great-grandmother had a dresser in the living room with a lot of trinkets, jewelry boxes, and statues of things people had given her on top of it.

Irma James (*middle, looking at camera*) with friends at a juke joint, courtesy of Loren Phillips.

I would sit there and I'd ask her, "Where did this come from?" Or, "Where did this come from?" I just kept asking her questions. I was just inquisitive. She would sit there and eat her vanilla wafers and answer the questions.

I got a piece of paper, and started writing down every one in the family that she would name—my great grandfather, his sisters, her sister, her cousins. Her parents came from Chicago. They were actually in New Orleans first. Her mother was a slave in New Orleans, so she was one generation from being a slave.

But New Orleanians had more freedom than any other cities. New Orleans was more European. Even slaves back then had more freedoms, because they didn't have to work on Sundays. They were able to go to Congo Square to practice their religion—they weren't stripped of their religion. And that's why New Orleanians today have more culture.

New Orleans was a main port for slaves, and most of the slaves that came in through New Orleans were coming in from the Greater and Lower Antilles, where they had been taken to break them. Then they would bring them in, and then sell them in the French Quarter. The ones that remained developed relationships with the French and the Spaniards and the Indians. And that's one of the reasons we look the way we look and we speak the way we speak. We don't speak with Southern drawls, like most Southerners.

Irma: They called us people of color.

Kenneth: I was about to ask that.

Loren: They knew they had some level of black in them, so they would call them "people of color." They could have been black people who were mixed with French, black people who were mixed with Spanish, black people who were mixed with Native American.

Kenneth: I didn't know any of this.

Loren: And they don't teach it, which is really sad because it would give people more pride in this city, and it would give people more pride in themselves. During my mom's time, kids actually sat down and listened to family stories. That's an African heritage—it was how the history of the family was passed on.

Irma: A lot of times, we used to get together on the weekend, and they'll give suppers and sell fried fish or fried chicken for 50 cents. You got to know a lot of your neighbors that way.

Loren: Like that was the purpose of the family reunions, so you could meet the new generation. My great grandfather was Joseph Miles. He grew up between LaPlace and New Orleans.

Irma: Nanan Sesine's house was right on the edge of LaPlace. You had to go across rail road tracks to purchase the vegetables, the greens, and so forth.

Loren: A lot of them were still sharecroppers, and then a lot of them actually owned land. My great grandfather was a Mason. Later we learned that Miles was not his real last name. His last name was Fourous and he was of Haitian descent. He got in some trouble and changed his name before moving to New Orleans. It was here he met my great-grandmother.

Kenneth: I'm listening cause I'm gonna think of my follow-up questions.

Loren: The follow-up questions are always anything that you're interested in hearing, or you think someone else is interested in hearing. You can't be afraid to ask a question. The only thing the person being interviewed can say is, "I refuse to answer it." And you just figure out a very smart way of going around it and ask the question again in a different way.

Kenneth: I can't think of anything right now. I'll just listen.

Loren: My great-grandfather spoke French—a *patois*—and I never got to meet him. He died of cardiac arrest the year before I was born.

Irma: You know, in our family, we could go down the line and find out we have relatives who are really Caucasians.

Loren: Like Irma's ex-husband, his mother looks Mexican. She looks like a Mexican. And they're very short.

Kenneth: Well, how does your ex-husband look?

Loren: Like the devil.

Kenneth: He—oh. [*Laughter*]

Loren: He looks South American—he's lighter than me. He has more yellow tones in his skin. High cheekbones.

Family History

When my Aunt Loren spoke on the Native Americans, Haitians, and the Creoles, I couldn't believe how many different cultures there were in our family. That's something to think about—all those bloodlines coming through my dark brown skin and thick, black, wavy hair.

In elementary school, I was taught that my family was from Africa, and I assumed we were pure Black African Americans. But some of my family members' features were different. My uncle Frederick had long, thick hair and I thought he looked like an Indian.

In school, there were only a few people who looked mixed. Jermaine was a grade higher than me. He had real long, wavy hair he wore in a plait down his back. One time I walked into the bathroom, saw his hair and said, "Girls ain't supposed to be in here."

He turned around, "I'm not a girl!"

I told him, "Oh, my bad."

Besides these physical clues, I never had a connection with any of my family's background, and I still don't because I am not around them as much as I want to be. When I was younger, I liked going into Spider's corner store on St. Bernard and Milton because the owners spoke Spanish, and I loved listening to the different sounds. I thought the Spanish words might have been English words pronounced backwards.

It wasn't until eighth grade that I had a white teacher—Ms. Ferris. She taught first period math class, and had also taught my brothers. Sometimes the students would call her a white bitch and other combinations that included white as a negative. I asked them, "What is it that you have against white people?" They still have racism going on, but it makes no sense to judge people by their skin color. I

Irma Phillips (*middle right*) with her husband, courtesy of Loren Phillips.

try to talk to people of different colors. I would like to know more about what they enjoy doing. What do they eat? What kind of things are they learning in school?

Loren's pictures of our family were shocking to me. When I saw pictures of my great, great-grandmother I didn't know what to think. They were dressed in their high heel shoes, dresses, matching gloves with a nice hair style—the way a classy older lady should dress. I finally saw a picture of my grandpa, Mr. Lewis Phillips, too.

Terrance told me he hadn't seen Grandpa since he was five. When we were young, he used to draw pictures to help Kimani and me get a sense of what he looked like. He always drew him with curly hair. Recently, Terrance went with my mama to see him. Terrance reported that he looks like Loren and Irvin—that he is short and does have curly hair. I can't wait until I meet him. It will be my first time. I wonder if he knew when Kimani and I were born. We'll meet one day, and maybe he could tell me about himself and our family.

Mama Dot in her garden in the St. Bernard, courtesy of Irma Phillips.

TAKE IT APART

Kenneth: What was it like growing up in the St. Bernard?

Loren: It was actually completely different from what it is now cause there was more a sense of community. People actually took pride to the point where the bottom floor apartments had gardens, and they were maintained. Everybody knew each other. It wasn't a question of, "Who are those kids and what are they doing back here?" We knew to come in when it started getting dark. When the streetlights came on, you had to be on your porch, and God forbid if your mom had to come and look for you. She would beat you and embarrass you in front of the other kids.

Irma: It was really disciplined then. Strict parents.

Loren: I was in the third grade when we moved in. So, how old are you when you're in the third grade?

Irma: You were seven or eight.

Loren: We were excited because we were moving into a bigger apartment, and then we knew we were going to be able to walk to my aunt's house and be near our cousins. And then there were other people to get to know. I was more introverted, so I was just excited about the apartment, not too excited about other people.

Kenneth: What was Uncle Irv like?

Loren: Aggravating sometimes because he always had to find something to get into.

Irma: He used to love to take things apart and put it back together.

Loren: Yeah, especially if it was electronic, he would take it apart. And if it was yours, he wouldn't ask you if he could do it. You would just come back and learn that it was done.

I call it hood engineering; he was good with it. [*Laughter*] He had a short attention span. But he was closer to Lynette, to your mom, because they were the youngest. He would have been 41.

Irma: Yeah, he's still 41.

Loren: DJing.

Irma: He's on a heavenly tour.

Kenneth: You know what Kimani told me? He said, "Y'all wonder if Uncle'll be DJing for God?" I said to him, "I don't know." [*Laughter*]

Irma: After grandfather died, I cried so much and I was so angry. I said, "Lord, why did you take my grandpa?" My grandmother said, "Don't question the Lord." I said, "Okay." She said, "The reason why God took your grandfather is because he loves him more than we can ever love him."

Loren: I think it's cool to question God.

Irma: I questioned him.

Loren: I question him every day.

Irma: And she said, "He wanted your grandfather-home with him." I said, "Okay." And I was so angry.

Loren: But Irvin was cool. One thing I can honestly say, if he had something, he would share. If you asked him to, he would share it. Now, your mom, on the other hand, was a completely different person.

Kenneth: What was my mom like?

Loren: Aggravating.

[*Laughter*]

Irma: She was on the tomboy side.

Loren: Yeah, and mean.

Irma: She used to love to play football.

Loren: She was the baby, and she was closer to Irvin. You couldn't tell her nothing. Or she would pretend she was on your side, and then she'd rat on you. [*Laughter*]

Irma: Siblings.

Kenneth: Why did y'all fight?

Loren: Just children. "That's mine, don't touch it." Then we'd fight over it.

Irma: Or "I'm watching this on the television."

Loren: On Saturdays, we'd watch karate movies, then go outside and do the whole karate thing with some of the other kids. You can tell everybody watched the same movie, because we'd all meet in the driveway and do everything that we saw on television.

Kenneth: What kind of music did you like when you were growing up?

Loren: My taste in music was very, very eclectic. The first song that I remember was Stevie Wonder, "Signed, Sealed, Delivered." I fell in love with Stevie Wonder, Diana Ross, and the Shirelles. I loved all the Motown classics—to this day, I still listen to them. I listened to Fleetwood Mac, the Beatles.

Kenneth: The Beatles?

Loren: I like rock and roll. I listened to Jimi Hendrix. I loved Jimi Hendrix. And one of my favorites was Janis Joplin. I would just listen to cassettes of Janis Joplin.

Kenneth: Who is she?

Loren: She was a rock and roll singer from Texas, and she had this raspy, raspy voice. When she would sing, it was just so soulful and so strong that you'd connect to it. I have it in my car; I still listen to it. You would like Janis Joplin.

Kenneth: I like Whitney Houston.

Loren: You'd like Janis Joplin more, especially "Cry, Cry Baby," you'd love it. She died too young.

Kenneth: I'll listen to it one day. When did you move to New Orleans East?

Loren: To New Orleans East? Actually, I was living in Gentilly first, and I decided to move closer to my office out there in the East. I found an apartment that was like one exit from our office.

Kenneth: How was it different from the St. Bernard?

Loren: I was in college at University of New Orleans, and I was still living in the St. Bernard in my 20s. I had found an apartment that was gated, and I convinced my mom that it was nice, and it was safe. And it was near the university. It was scary cause that was the first time I had lived by myself. Lynette and Irvin are the youngest; they were already living on their own, although when they moved out, they moved out with someone. I was moving by myself.

Kenneth: How did Uncle Irvin get involved in music?

Loren: My uncle Robert gave me—you know the little portable turntables?

Kenneth: Oh, yeah.

Loren: In the late 1970s, we must have been like ten, and Irvin took that and turned it into a DJ thing. That's why I say he would take your stuff and use it. [*Laughter*]

And he took the speakers loose from my mom's stereo, and connected them to that, and he would DJ. He'd been doing that since before I even heard of a DJ. He always loved hip-hop—he would take a Michael Jackson or Stevie Wonder album and find a way to weave them into a hip-hop song—scratch them into each other. But it would be my albums! [*Laughter*] That's when the fights would start.

The only thing we had heard that was close to hip-hop was—what's that album you bought us? The "Macaroni Wood" [*Singing*] *The chicken tastes like wood, dunt duh.* Mia knows it. I could ask Mia. Can you pause that for a second?

[*Calls Mia X*]

Loren: It was the Sugar Hill Gang, it was around that time. And we had the wax, the vinyl. He was still working from what we used to call record boxes, because it was the stereo inside of a box, and he would scratch on those.

Growing up with Irvin, it didn't register to me how other people felt about his work. He was just Irvin to me. Other people thought it was interesting. I

DJ Irv in the St. Bernard, courtesy of Loren Phillips.

thought it was annoying. At that time, I was into classical music, so anything outside of classical music or Motown was annoying to me. But I love poetry, and I thought it was kinda like poetry to a beat.

Kenneth: What were the DJs like back in the day?

Loren: Very, very innovative. The DJs today, everything's digital. A lot of them bring their laptops into clubs. It's like, "What purpose do you serve?" Back then, everything was analog so they had to think. They had to be creative and they were more experimental. If something didn't sound right, they tried something else until it sounded good to their ears. I applaud DJs from back then.

In the St. Bernard, I remember they would DJ from the balconies, and people would come out for block party in the courtyards. And Irvin was one of those DJs. He was one of the first to sample other kids of music besides hip-hop. He would fuse the two. Actually, I have a picture of him right before he was killed; he was DJing in one of the courtyards.

I think the first thing that turned me off was Eazy-E. I was in the backseat of a car with Irvin and one of his friends. Irvin was sitting in the front, and they were playing something by Eazy-E, and I heard the song, and I just was like, "Ugh, if that's rap music, I don't like it." And then one day I was with my girlfriend, walking from Gentilly to the St. Bernard, and somebody was passing in a car blaring Salt-n-Pepa's, "I'll Take Your Man." And I said, "Oh, I like that." She said, "That's hip-hop." And we called the radio station to get them to play the whole song, and we went and bought the little 45 of it. I fell in love with hip-hop when I heard that. I really liked East Coast because it wasn't overpowered by the beat. I got to hear the lyrics, and it was more poetic.

Irvin, on the other hand, was interested in anything with a good beat—anything. It could be hip-hop; it could be jazz; it could be R&B; it could be rock and roll. If it was something that had a good hook, he would take that hook and sample it into something. I would drop him off on Fridays at a place called Ghost Town in Hollygrove where he DJ'd. He just started this thing where he sampled the Showboys' beat (what they call Triggerman now) and put it with Brown's beat. And this guy named MC T.T. Tucker jumped on the stage when he heard Irvin mixing the two and started chanting. The audience went crazy and that became like a ritual. They did it like every Friday.

DJ Irv and MC T.T. Tucker, courtesy of Loren Phillips.

If they knew Irvin was DJing somewhere, that's where people went. And everybody just started dancing. It became more erotic and you really got to see more of New Orleans island heritage—it was more Caribbean, the way people would dance. But no one looked at it like, "What are you doing?" But it's more like, "Okay, how are you doing this? Show me how you're doing it."

This producer thought it would be interesting to record it because there was no sound like that at that time. Irvin came and sat down and told me about it. It still wasn't registering with me because I was listening to Nina Simone. I'm driving to school, and he said, "Would you be my manager?" And I'd never worked with anyone in that capacity, and I said, "I

guess so." I went to the library and did the research on what a manager was required to do. The most important thing to me was the income. I needed to know, "How I'm gonna be compensated?" I don't want a title; titles don't excite me.

I went in the studio with them. I remember sitting down with one of the guys who was producing it, and wanting to know what my brother was getting from it—what his contract was because there was no major distribution company. Everything was placed on consignment. I wanted a copy of every consignment sheet to make sure that he was being compensated. They recorded that song, "Where Dey At" in one take. Irvin was actually DJing during the recording.

The single was released in December 1991. Davey Dee said, "You have to hear this song. We have to put it on the air." And they put it on the air, and immediately it became highly requested. And they started copying it. It went to disc makers to be duplicated.

That was the birth of bounce. You could see someone in their car, and you'd know they were listening to "Where Dey At," because they knew the lyrics. Tucker and Irvin incorporated a bit of politics. David Duke was on the scene at the time, and people were so frustrated with David Duke that Tucker incorporated that into the lyrics of the song. I think it afforded people an opportunity to get their frustrations out. People would chant even harder when the song was playing.

DJ Jimi came after them and re-recorded the song. He was picked up by another label, so it was easier for him to get it out to the masses. With Irvin and Tucker, it was more regional—New Orleans, Mississippi, Texas. I used to go on tour with them.

I remember receiving a call from Luke from 2 Live Crew. He was interested in signing them. He flew me and one of the producers out to Miami to entertain us. When we got in the board room, it must have been a 75 page contract and I questioned everything in there. The other producer became frustrated, and I said, "Well, I'm sorry, this is my brother. I'm not going to sell him off to some producer and have him lose everything." We flew back to New Orleans without a contract being signed. I sat down with Irvin and explained to him why I did it, because he was frustrated also. I had to show them the loopholes in the contract where they would lose all of their rights to ownership.

T. Tucker And
D.J. IRV Coming At Ya!

United Visions Production Co., Inc.
New Orleans, La.
(504) 282-3685

Publicity photograph, by Loren Phillips.

I still own the rights to it. I'd say about a few years ago, I saw Juvenile in Texas. He came to me and asked if it was okay to sample it and I gave him permission. It was brought to my attention that a lot of people had sampled the song, but it was just too much to deal with, trying to go after people and put your life back in order after Katrina.

Kenneth: What was it like for you when my uncle Irvin went to jail?

Loren: He went to jail in July of 1992. I think he felt helpless more than anything, and scared like, "I'm away from my family, away from home." I deal with tragedies a lot different than most people. I block stuff out as if it doesn't exist. I tried to be supportive for my mom, but I didn't completely understand why he was incarcerated.

85

I would write to him, and he would write back. Then he would get frustrated because I didn't respond in a timely manner. He wanted a dictionary to write. I went to the UNO bookstore and got the thesaurus, a dictionary, and a spelling book. We sent that to him. And he sent me some scarves that he had actually drawn with ink pens.

Irma: Handkerchiefs.

Loren: This artwork he did with ink pens, and it was just so interesting. He wanted me to sell them. And I just couldn't do it cause I felt like it was his work and wanted him to do a lot of things on his own. I didn't want him to be handicapped.

Kenneth: And all of us went by Grandma's house when he got out.

Loren: My sister, his friend Dion, and I went to pick him up, and immediately he went right back into DJing at Prime Time on the weekends. And he loved fashion, so he was right back into fashion. He didn't miss a beat. I think people had missed him so much to the point where they were buying him clothes and buying equipment for him to get him back into the swing of things.

We kept him abreast of the new artists, because we'd send him music. And his fellow inmates, they probably got music from their family members. At first, I didn't understand the whole chant to music, and that was my ignorance. After doing the research on it, I've come to see it as an African tradition. It all goes back to Congo Square. I think unconsciously they drew from that. They didn't know they were drawing from that, but it was music to message.

Kenneth looking at artwork Irvin made in prison, by Rachel Breunlin.

It became a New Orleans thing. Like every region in the U.S. has it's own style. You could differentiate East Coast from West Coast. You could differentiate Texas style from Louisiana style. When you think of people like Hurricane Chris, it's almost like they can sing and they're rapping so there's not a break in phrasing when they do chant a rap. But then these people like Soulja Boy and other similar artists adopted the whole bounce style and tried to coin it as their own. It's nothing but bounce music. I just hate the fact that they don't credit New Orleans for that. They don't credit New Orleans at all.

WRITING

Kenneth: How did you get interested in writing?

Loren: My mom. She used to give me books before I went to kindergarten. She wrote poetry. I would write stories that rhyme. And because I was the first child, my mom would spend more time teaching me how to write, how to read.

Kenneth: What was your role in *Da R.U.D.E.* magazine?

Loren: I owned it; I created it. It was supposed to be a pamphlet for a convention in Atlanta. I was asked to come together with a group of guys. They knew I was a reporter and I was good at writing. I went around and I interviewed the local recording artists in my car. It was supposed to be a one-page flyer with the recording artist on it, and we were going to Jack the Rapper in Atlanta with it to give people an idea of what New Orleans' music was about. Before we knew it, we had 25 pages, and it was a magazine. I published it for 15 years.

I did everything myself. I would work from two in the afternoon until four in the morning because I was just that passionate about it. I taught myself all of the programs, from Quark to Photoshop. I went around to different companies and asked them if they were interested in advertising and I did a barter system.

I got to a point where I was eating pasta for months. I would buy the 69 cent pack of spaghetti, the big old box, and I would just add salt and pepper and celery, or do one with parsley or butter just to make sure the magazine was taken care of. It was just a sacrifice—it was my baby. One time, I was so involved in

Tupac Shakur interviewed by Loren Phillips, courtesy of Loren Phillips.

the magazine, I didn't have enough money to print it. I pawned the computer and got the money to print the magazine. And once the magazine was sold, I went and got my computer back.

Kenneth: That was smart.

Loren: Yeah. I drove around with boxes in the back of my car and went to the record stores, the music stores like Musicland, and Blockbuster had music at the time. They would call me back and say, "We sold out, can you bring some more?" And I'd say, "Can you cut me a check?" And they were like, "We have to contact corporate cause we don't do checks from here." And I said, "Well, you need to, because I need to pay for the cost of this magazine."

Kenneth: What was it like writing about the music scene in New Orleans?

Loren conducting an interview, courtesy of Loren Phillips.

Loren : I got to meet a lot of people. I had heard this song by a female artist. She was a local artist, and I liked her because there weren't any local female artists in the city. I said, "I like her sound. I like the poetry behind it." Her flow was smooth. I remember a producer coming to me, asking me if I would write a story on Mia X. I told him, "The only way I'd do it is if you introduce me to her." The next day, he brought her by. It was just a good energy, a spiritual thing. We connected like we had known each other 20 years. I think one of the reasons Mia and I have remained friends to this day is because we both got to see each other go through our personal trials.

She had belonged to a group called New York Incorporated, and had made a name for herself, but she trusted me and asked me to be her manager. I can honestly say once she became a part of No Limit, she brought me in. She's one that if you do something for her, she's not going to forget it. Mia appeared on three covers of the magazine and she was always actively involved in getting advertisers and making sure that No Limit advertised with me. And Master P always paid. He was very generous.

My Brief Encounter with Mia X

Mia X is my favorite rapper. The first time I heard her voice I said, "Man! Who is that?" Terrance said, "That's Mia X. She raps with Master P—No Limit." I said, "For real?"

I saw her in "I Got The Hook Up." She was my favorite part in that movie.

One day, I was at my house and I handcuffed my legs together. I couldn't find the key. I tried everything—screwdriver, knives, spoons and forks. My mom called Loren and asked did she have something to open handcuffs. Loren walked into the room and I saw somebody else with her. I thought it was my mother.

Loren asked me, "K, do you know who this is?"

I said, "Mia X?"

Then Mia said, "Hey Kenneth."

I started crying because I couldn't believe it was really my favorite rapper. She talked just the way she rapped.

That was my first time meeting a celebrity. Kimani said, "Every time No Limit's video comes on, Kenneth always rap your part."

Don't Start No Shit, Won't be no Shit...

Mia X's publicity photo sent to DJ Irv while he was in prison, courtesy of Irma Phillips.

REPRESENTATION

Loren: After my brother's death, I became a recluse. I was asked to do an interview on New Orleans hip hop by Nik Cohn for a European magazine. Later on, I found out he wrote a book, *Tricksta*. I didn't authorize him to put me in a book. Certain things he wrote were on point. For instance, when he said I sit an extra plate at a table when I'm eating by myself for those who can't afford to eat, and for those who aren't here any more.

The way he described me was almost like this goddess, and then right after that, tore me up. It was defamation of character. The book to me is completely sensationalized, and it's an ugly picture of the local scene.

Kenneth: What do you think about me writing a book?

Loren: I think it's a great thing, writing the book. And even having the ability to do so, the resources to do so. I'm just glad people still read. I like the whole idea of the library, honestly.

Irma: I'm very proud of you.

Loren: I'm hoping that you use this book to get any and everything out. When you don't voluntarily let something out, it will find a way to come out in another relationship, or just when it's not expected. You see people who snap and go off. I always tell people, "Whatever the situation is, I think it's good to write it down." Even if you write a letter to that person telling them, "This is how you make me feel," and then tear it up afterwards. Then you've gotten that out—you've given birth to whatever you're feeling at that time.

You can put in anything that you feel comfortable sharing. That's the only thing: You have to be comfortable. Once it's there, it's there. You can't remove it. It's done.

Kenneth and Loren, by Rachel Breunlin.

You Have to Be Comfortable

My life feels like a fat man trying to climb over a hill. The things that I do and I say—I know it's mean. I wake up in the morning mad because I don't like the things I have to wake up to.

I'm not trying to take that thuggish route that my grandfather and dad took. I want to follow my own dreams and my own route. A long time ago, this lady named Ms. Cheryl stayed right across the driveway from us. Sometimes I would go and sit downstairs and tell her how much I liked church. She would tell me, "You have a great future ahead of you. Don't let nothing drag you down in life. The devil could never win unless you let him."

The real question is: Who am I? My name is not Kenneth Randel Phillips. I'm not 16 years old. I was not born June 4, 1992. Somebody, please, tell me who I am.

Gemini: Split personality. I'm always mad. This is an everyday thing—maybe stressing and don't even know it. My fists ball up too much. Whoever I look at becomes the target. It's like I have noises inside my head, just speaking all at one time.

Every time I say something to my mama, I know she must be thinking "Where did this boy get this stuff from?" I'll sit down and sing Whitney Houston's "I Have Nothing." I really like the song, but then I get mad all over again. I just need a day to find out who I really am. I just got to take my time to get to know me. There's no other way for me to do it.

Lynette Phillips, courtesy of Irma Phillips.

VI. Interview with My Mother, Lynette Phillips

My mama goes by the name "Net." She has short hair, brown skin, and is five foot seven with light freckles and pretty dark brown eyes. She loves purses and likes to dress in jeans and fitted shirts. My mama is a Gemini like me. She can be cool with you, or curse you out. She has only has a few close friends and family members. She's trustworthy.

We watch T.V., play cards, and go shopping together. Always about her business, working and taking care of me and my brothers, she wants the best for us.

If I have to tell her something, I wait for a day when she's smiling and happy. My mama has to really be calm to be able to hear hard things because she doesn't talk about her feelings very much. That's why I think we have our best talks when we're walking. We'll talk about the relationships in our family, school, jobs.

I know she worries about me because I'm not like my brothers. I like to hang out with girls, but I don't have a girlfriend. She's concerned that I look at things differently.

It was difficult to find time to do this interview because my mama is always working. We made time on a Saturday afternoon after she got off work at the hotel. She was in a good mood and talked about her playing football, dancing at DJs, our relationship with my dad, and how strict she's been on us. It wasn't a long walk, but we ended up getting some good talking done.

Lynette in her apartment in the St. Bernard,
courtesy of Lynette Phillips.

Kenneth: All right. What type of family did
you have?

Lynette: My mama's a real nice, sweet lady. She
helped a lot of people out work-wise. My father, he
doesn't exist. I mean, he never was there for me.
Until recently, I hadn't seen him since my oldest son
was a week old. That's been nineteen years.

Kenneth: What did your mama do for a living?

Lynette: She was a secretary for a doctor's office
over there at Bynum's store and a lot of people loved
her. A lot of people were real hurt when she stopped
working there. She had problems with her legs. She
gave it up and started dealing with my grandmother
when she had a stroke a couple of years ago. She's still
dealing with my grandmother.

Kenneth: What did you want to be when you
grew up?

L: Well, I thought about police work but you had to
go through too much to be a policewoman. I thought
about being a physical therapist, to help out people who are rebuilding their strength. I had to go
through therapy when I hurt my ankle at work. I've
been doing housekeeping 11 years now, and I'm tired
of housekeeping.

Kenneth: What did you like most about going
to school?

Lynette: Eating lunch. My best subject was
science. I'm not too good at math. I loved PE.

Kenneth: Did you finish school?

Lynette: No.

Kenneth: Why not?

Lynette: The reason why I didn't finish is because I
was pregnant at a young age. It's something I could
have done—gone back to school—but I had responsibilities then. During the time when I did get pregnant, I was going to a trade school for janitorial work
at Goodwill on Jeff Davis. They show you how to go
through different hotels and hospitals and learn how
to clean. It was just a class for me to go to until I got
a steady job.

Terrance was a year old when I went back to doing
janitorial work at Brother Martin High School.
That's when I got my own apartment. That job lasted
for eight months and then I moved on to other housekeeping positions.

Kenneth: How did you act when you found out
you were pregnant?

Lynette (*left*) as a teenager in the St. Bernard, courtesy of Loren Phillips.

Kenneth: When you were younger, did Grandma talk to you about sex?

Lynette: Yes, when I was getting up in age. It was time for your parents to start talking to you about sex or you go to your parent and you talk to your parent about sex.

Kenneth: Did you always want boys?

Lynette: To be honest, when I first got pregnant I prayed to have a boy. I knew what I put my parents through as a girl. He blessed me with three boys. It really didn't matter what I had, a girl or a boy really, as long as they were healthy.

CATCHING UP

Kenneth: What happened after Kimani fell out the window?

Lynette: I had the window in the kitchen airing out. The screen was on the window. His big head pushed the screen loose. I told him to stay away, and went back to washing dishes. Next thing you know, I looked back and the whole screen and him were gone. I ran out. I didn't care if water was running. I ran down the steps. I really don't know if I picked him up or the ambulance did.

They rushed him to the hospital. He fell straight on his back and his head. I thought he would bust something, but thank the Lord he didn't break anything and Child Protective Services didn't fault me for anything.

I thought it affected him because it was really hard for him to relate to things—like as far as when the teacher asked him something or when he came home

Lynette: I mean, I was frustrated a little because I knew I wasn't ready for it. I knew who my child's father was. It's not like I had to go pinpoint. As long as I knew he was gonna be there for me and my child, I just dealt with it.

Kenneth: How did Grandma react when you told her you were pregnant?

Lynette: She wasn't mad or anything like that. She told me now I had responsibilities. Some moms would want to put you out but I didn't have that type of parent. She was always there for me—even with my other kids.

and did his homework. It's good for every child to take his time, but you or Terrance were always having to help him. I always wanted him to try on his own and then the teachers were telling me he needed to be evaluated. I was telling them about the fall he had and they said there was nothing they could do about it.

They were working with him, and after a while he finally began to catch up. Now I don't have any problem with him doing his homework. He'll sit down and do it. I say, "Kimani, I'm going to have Kenny or Terrance check your homework," and everything will be all right.

Kenneth: I don't like talking about it. Of course I help him —he's my brother! Ma, do you think that's why I'm protective of him?

Lynette: Yeah, in a way.

Kenneth: Ma, you know how Kimani is—he's just nice though, right?

Lynette: Yeah, he's a sweetheart.

Kenneth: But you look at Kimani walk through that door and if you didn't know him at all you'd probably be like, "Oh, this a gangster."

Lynette: It's just the way he dresses. It's not that he's sagging. Some little boys like to have their pants low, but I don't really play that. He does that when I'm not around. But it's just the way he dresses.

Kenneth: And acts sometimes.

Lynette: Some ways he acts, but it's just a little mind thing. It's not that he wants to be that. He loves rap music. Some kids pick that up from rap, but he's not gonna be a gangster in here. A lot of people compliment me on my kids.

Kenneth: What did you enjoy most about your childhood?

Lynette: I used to play football a lot. It was like a little tomboy thing. We were girls against the boys. I loved football, still love football.

Kenneth: Yeah, let me ask you this. Why is it important for me to learn how to play football?

Lynette: I think every child, every little boy, should want to play some type of ball—especially football. And you're sized to play football, too. Everybody tells me that. I told them Kimani played quarterback there for Willie Hall.

Kenneth: That was a long time ago, though.

Lynette: But you need to play football.

Kenneth: I don't.

Lynette: I could watch it all day. It doesn't just have to be NFL. It could be college.

Kenneth: If I sat a big T.V. in the middle of the street, you would sit up there and watch it if it had football on it. I could be watching a good T.V. show and you come in and kick us out and put the football game on.

Lynette: Hey, you already know what time of day it is.

Football in My Family

My mama used to say, "Look at him, he don't know nothing about football," trying to make me mad. I didn't, and I still don't, know anything about the game.

There was the time when I was eleven and Kimani was ten, and we went to football practice together at Willie Hall. They had a routine where one group was tackling, one was throwing, and one was catching. I got picked in the catching group, which was impossible for me. They sent me out to catch thirty times. The ball hit me in my face a few times, I missed a few more, and a couple of times it hit my hands. I didn't catch any of them.

The coach paired me with a quarterback to give me a chance to work on the skill one-on-one. I didn't improve. The coach thought I wasn't putting in enough effort. I was frustrated, so I walked off the field. Kimani stood there and just looked at me leaving.

When he came home, Kimani was still laughing at me. He asked if I wanted to come back to the team. I said no, but he went upstairs, got our football, and took me out to the driveway. He kept pitching the ball to me—normal at first but increasing in speed until we got to a throw we call "the bullet." It comes at you hard and fast.

I was catching all of them, and Kimani said, "Well, now you want to catch the ball," acting like I was

Terrance, Kenneth, and Kimani in their Saints jerseys, courtesy of Lynette Phillips.

messing up on purpose at practice. The truth was, I was kind of shy to play in front of people, and though I can catch, I still only play with Kimani, Willie, and Eugene.

My mom still teases me, but we also play. Mostly pitch and catch, although sometimes we play hot potato—trying to get rid of the football as quickly as possible.

TO EACH THEIR OWN

Kenneth: When you were growing up you hung with boys. Had you ever had a problem with somebody calling you a tomboy?

Lynette: No, not really. We played ball—Gibson Court against Jumonville Court. It just was a fun thing to do.

Kenneth: I think your generation is different than ours.

Lynette: They'll look at the girl wanting to be a tomboy and think she'll wind up a lesbian or if a boy acts like a girl, he'll wind up gay. You know, to each his own. They said things about Keith, but his mom

Daphne and I never sat down and talked about anything. She goes and raises hers like she wants, and I'm gonna go raise mine.

Kenneth: When people used to say that about me, I used to get out and fight, but I have a better understanding now. I look past it. I don't have that problem anymore.

Lynette: You get wiser as you get older. You're trying to respect people whether they respect you. So all that comes together. I mean, bad nerves—that could get you in trouble. If you can't sit down and listen it really will.

Speak Up

Keith went to Bourbon Street for Decadence—the gay parade in the French Quarter. The next day he came by and pulled a pamphlet out of his pocket, and said, "Look what a church was passing out." On the front it said, "Heaven or Hell." When I looked inside, it said, "Homosexuality is a sin." I told him, "Get this stuff out my house." He was laughing, and I said, "That's not funny."

Keith and I have had a lot of encounters with the church. One time, we were standing in front of the Pentecostal Church with Bibles in our hand. Keith saw some girls jumping rope and went over to join in the double dutch. One girl said, "Get your gay ass from over here." Keith threw the Bible on the ground and he went to going off. I was about to join him, but then I said, "No it's not the time and place for this."

Another time in the St. Bernard, a traveling pastor was setting up chairs and speakers in the field in the back of our driveway. He was wearing a Jheri Curl and a black suit. We were passing by and Keith was talking loud. The man told Keith he was a disgrace. Keith ran, took the microphone, jumped on one of the chairs, and started preaching back, "Sir, you are a disgrace!! You came in here to preach to these people and you don't even know me!"

In school, we dealt with it as well. I was walking the hallways at school and the disciplinarian was calling Keith out of a classroom. The teacher said, "That's why I would rather work with real boys." Keith said,

"Don't play with me." It wasn't the first time I had heard a teacher say homophobic comments. When one student was talking about his boyfriend and the teacher said, "Uh uh! We don't need that kind of talk in here." She pulled out her Bible and followed the boy into another classroom. He said, "You don't need to tell me how I live my life." She brought up Jesus. "Is Jesus living my life?"

"No, he's giving you life."

"Well, there's a difference between giving me life and living my life."

I hate it when people say you're going to hell if you're gay. I feel like people should be able to love who they want to love. If it wasn't made to be like that, it wouldn't be like that. It's hard to find people in my life who are open-minded.

In tenth grade, my PE teacher, Ms. Brooks, was doing a unit on sex education. Someone asked, "What if they're gay?" I was wondering what she was going to say because I knew one of her sons was gay. She was sitting down at her desk. She took off her glasses, stood up, and walked to the front. She sat on the edge with her legs crossed, and said, "My son is gay. And I will love him whether he's straight or gay. I'm gonna love him because he's my son."

There was silence in the room. I wanted to get up and give her a hug because you can't find too many parents who will speak up for their child.

REAL CLOSE

Kenneth: Were you and Irvin similar to me and Kimani in how close we are?

Lynette: Yeah.

Kenneth: Could you explain what y'all's relationship
was like?

Lynette: Me and Irvin, we did a lot of things together. We went to the clubs where he used to DJ and sometimes I used to help him after he cut hair. I swept up for him and he gave me five dollars. We played ball together. We just were real close. It really hurt me when they killed him. I lost him in 2001. It was some dealing with a dice game.

Kenneth: It was a shock. Weren't you about to jump out the window?

Lynette: What window? No, I wasn't about to jump out the window—not no third floor window!

Kenneth: You were hanging off the window. I didn't know. I thought you were about to jump.

Lynette: He was really creative. He took hundreds of pieces of a baby doll house and put it together for me. He was an artist. But the thing he really enjoyed while he was on this earth was his music. It was his music. He was getting the name DJ Irv and he started DJing in Ghost Town and he did a few DJs in the St. Thomas Housing Project. Sometimes, he brought his music to my house, and played it with y'all. He used to always rib us and talk about how nappy my hair was.

Lynette and Irvin with their Aunt, courtesy of Irma Phillips.

Kenneth: Mine, too.

Lynette: He talked about Terrence's nose. He talked about how big Kimani's head was. He used to always say, "But I love my nephews." He went to jail in Houston. He did eight years, came home, and went back to the same woman and his music. You couldn't tell him nothing. He was in his own little world.

Irvin fixed his bed up real nice—his turn table on top of the bed. Once we heard the gunshots, my mama was calling him to see where he was. He wasn't answering his phone. She came by me. I was looking out the window, everybody was running saying, "That's Irvin! That's Irvin!" My mama panicked and tried to go round there, but the ambulance took him. Everybody rushed to the hospital and that was the end of everything; the end of everything. When I say people running and crying? He was loved. A lot of people loved him as DJ Irv.

Sometimes his son, Brandon, is so much like him. We sit around and talk about it. He misses his daddy, too. Even his ex-girlfriends. I just recently saw one, Allison, she was like, "Girl, DJ Irv, that was my baby."

BACK THAT THANG UP

Kenneth: What were people saying about the early bounce music? Do you know?

Lynette: We always listened to Irvin's CD. Everybody was getting on the walls dancing and popping.

Kenneth: You been dancing, Ma?

Lynette: I don't know how to dance like that. I make up my own dances and everybody's like, "Girl you doin them 1990s dances." I'll dance all night if it's the right type of hip hop.

Kenneth: What's your favorite?

Lynette: I think that was—

Kenneth: Jubilee?

Lynette: Yeah, I used to dance off of Jubilee and Juvenile, "Back That Thang Up." All of us—me, Leslie, LaVetha, Daphne (Keith's mom) and Ketha—used to be on the wall.

Kenneth: Oh how long ago was this?

Lynette: This was in 1998. We used to be bouncing in the St. Thomas Housing Project when DJ Jubilee performed.

Kenneth: Remember Dee used to "Back That Thang Up" in the kitchen?

Lynette: Oh Dee. Dee used to be the dance-around-man. He was real cool, didn't bother anybody. People used to throw sticks and bricks at him. We looked out for him cause he didn't really have nothing. He used to get a check, but whoever was getting it for him probably took it because they thought he'd go buy drugs or stuff he had no business buying.

Kenneth: I didn't know he was on drugs.

Lynette: Oh yeah, he had an overdose. He used to say, "All right, right, right, where Daphne at? Tell her I back that thang up for her, then give me a quarter." He used to be dancing for everybody.

Mr. Harrison's Sweetshop

It used to be so crowded. I used to hear all these voices in my ear. When I first walked in Mr. Harrison's Sweetshop, I was like, "I've never seen so much candy." He had everything you could think of: chocolates, Now-N-Laters, Mambos, Blow Pops, Starbursts, Skittles, M&M's, and the rest of that good stuff. That little building had almost 100 people trying to bunch up just to get inside, and I was one of them. Most of my money went straight to Mr. Harrison.

Every morning when I was in the third grade, I stopped at Mr. Harrison's for a dollar worth of watermelon candy for breakfast. It wasn't just me in the shop. The shop was right across the street from the project. Even after school I would go to the candy shop. After school everybody used to be in there. He had another worker named Raymond in there. I would stand in a 30 minute line just for some candy. But then he just shut down. One day after school we went to go and sign the building with highlighters. I know it sounds crazy but we did it.

Dee was also one of the workers at Mr. Harrison's. He put me out once because I was fussing with this lady who tried to skip the line. Dee said, "Get ya ass out! You don't talk to no adult like that." Everybody started laughing because of the way he talked.

I used to see him in the project, too. He walked in the driveway with his white t-shirt with beer stains on it and his khaki pants that used to be covered with mud. I remember he used to come up to the porch. He was the slowest walker I know. My mama would be sitting with friends and say, "Wuz up Dee!" And he'd say. "It ain't nothin, baby."

Dee, courtesy of Lynette Phillips.

Dee would always ask my mama, "You cook?" because at Mr. Harrison's he only worked for a cold drink. My mama would say, "Yeah. You hungry, Dee? Show us your dance."

Sometimes when I used to see him, I'd give him a dollar because that's what he would always ask for. One day I saw Dee and one of the workers fussing at Spider's. They thought Dee was trying to steal a bag of chips. One of the workers told Dee, "I better not catch you around here no more." Dee looked like he wanted to cry. He was standing up there looking like, "What did I do?" All I could think was, "I wish I could help you."

The last time I saw Dee he was in the Foy court and I gave him a quarter. He was looking so sad. It was like he had nothing to live for. That was the last time I saw Dee.

R.I.P. Dee

COULDN'T LIVE LIKE THAT

Kenneth: How did you meet my dad?

Lynette: I met your daddy in 1990, when I was 18. Terrance was a year old. He was hanging around my grandmother's house on 1515 Galvez. He knew my uncle and conversation just started laying on. I was with him for 10½ years. He lied to me and told me he was a certain age and he wasn't. He told me he was about 18 years old and he was nothing but 16.

A week later, when I met his mom, I sat down and talked with her and she asked me, "Did he tell you how old he was?" I kind of figured that anyway because he was kind of childish.

Kenneth: What did you like about him?

Lynette: First of all, he had a job working at Dickie Brennan's over there on Iberville St., in the French Quarter.

Kenneth: Did he take care of himself?

Lynette: Yeah, he took care of himself. He was a very neat, clean person, kept himself well-dressed.

Kenneth: Did you and my dad have a good relationship?

Lynette: Yeah, when we first started out. The relationship was kind of wavy after a while, especially when you're undecided and play with people's feelings. You can't really do that.

When he gets on this other side, he has a bad attitude. I didn't notice he had a bad temper until one time we went to a bar and he was drinking. For some reason, he thought a guy was talking to me. He had a little conversation with the guy and then started shoving me. I'm like, "Oh no, he's going crazy." I left out the bar, went to his mama's house, told his mama what was going on, and she told me to do what I had to do. I left him alone. I told him I couldn't live like that.

I had you in 1992 and Kimani in 1993. He was incarcerated for two-and-a-half years, came home, got him another little job. I was thinking that everything was gonna be okay. That didn't work out. He just was about the streets and the streets weren't me.

Kenneth: Why did you and my dad choose to break up?

Lynette: Well, I'll put it like this. The reason why we broke up in 2000 was because he was seeing someone else. He got married in 2001, and that was it. I knew something was going on cause I was working a night shift—11 at night to seven a.m., and he was supposed to be picking me up and he never came. He never was home when he should have been home, and I just couldn't put myself through that anymore. When he did come home, he tried to start a little fuss with me, I guess so he could move on, and that's exactly what he did.

Dad's New Family

My dad moved to the Eighth Ward with Angie and her family. We didn't see him for awhile, and then one day my grandma told me he had gotten married. She said Kimani and I were supposed to be in the wedding, but we didn't know about the ceremony.

During Katrina, my dad's family evacuated to Florida and decided to stay. I went to visit two years later. It was very hard for Kimani and me because we are not used to being separated. My dad, Angie, and her family drove to Jacksonville. It was a long ride. I was wishing for a sign that would say, "You are in Florida" or something.

Sometimes I would see Angie's brother, Shannon. Even though he was living in Florida, he wanted to come back and always said, "Eighth Ward to the max!" He'd come by my room and say, "What's up, fool?" and give me good-looking shirts that seemed to cost a lot of money.

I didn't spend much time with my dad. He was always gone, but one night we had a card game with Angie and her daughter. We were playing for 50 cents. I got tipsy and it was the best night I had. My dad kept getting mad because he was losing and my stepmom and I were looking out for each other.

The night before I left, they gave me a "I'm going to miss you" party. I got drunk that night, too. I drank so much that I might have forgotten what happened. All I remember was dancing with my stepmother to old R&B. I woke up on the floor in the living room.

Loretta and Kenneth at his wedding, courtesy of Loretta Martin.

They were having another party that day. Before it even started, I had to leave and started to cry. At the airport, I gave my daddy a big hug. I hadn't seen my dad in so long and I barely had time to spend with him. While I was walking away, I looked back and he started crying because he didn't want me to leave either.

It was my first time in an airport. I didn't know you had to take off your shoes at the security check. I was looking like, "What the hell!" After all that, I had to find my gate and I asked for assistance. In New Orleans, I stood outside and called my mom to come and get me. They had me waiting with a big, heavy-ass bag. I could pick out my brother's walk from anywhere. When he saw me, he started running.

Lynette, Dewayne, and his mama Sandra, courtesy of Lynette Phillips.

IF HE GOT IT, YOU GOT IT

Kenneth: How did you meet Dewayne?

Lynette: I met Dewayne at a club uptown. I was kind of depressed so I said to Daphne, "Let's go out." We went out and got ourselves a few drinks at her husband's uncle's club, Club Do It.

They had these three guys sitting at a table. I was pretending that I wanted to sit down knowing I had my eye on this guy. I was like, "Can I put my jacket on your chair?" And he said, "Sure you can."

I was like, "What are you guys drinking?"

He told me Crown and 7 and asked, "You mind having a drink?" I said, "No, I'm drinking Budweiser."

Dewayne's friend thought I was looking at him, but I was looking at Dewayne. We exchanged numbers, but we were both working and couldn't see each other right then and there. He was living in the Calliope Public Housing Development. He took me out. We got together and I have been with him ever since.

Kenneth: The first time I saw Dewayne, he was so tall.

Lynette: I met Dewayne on January 26, 2001.

Kenneth: He was super tall. What is it like for him to be part of our family?

Lynette: You know, everybody's relationships have their ups and downs, but we still hung in there. If he got it, you got it. He loves to joke around, too.

Kenneth: It was cool having him live with us, though. It was fun.

Lynette: You know he was the only one Kobey listened to.

Kenneth: I know, he sure didn't listen to me.

Lynette: When he heard that whistle, that's a rap. He know who it is.

Kenneth: I used to play fight with you and he would bark at us.

Lynette: Mhm. One time, Dewayne and I had just come in from work, and you were in the kitchen. I started looking for the chili and it was gone. I said, "Kobey, who did it?" Kobey looked right at you. Dewayne said, "I knew it, I knew it. Lil Kenny, what'd you do?"

Kenneth: I made chili with eggs.

Lynette: Kobey ratted on you, too.

Dewayne

I met Dewayne in the third grade a few months after my dad left for good. I was coming home from a hard day at school and walked in through the front door screaming "Ma!" Somebody was standing in front of her, but I couldn't see him because I was too far away. I walked into the kitchen and saw a man who was so tall, his head was on top of the cereal boxes. My mama said, "Don't you have manners?"

I said, "How you doing?" Then he said, "What's up lil man?" My mama said, "This is Dewayne."

I wouldn't say he took my daddy's place, but he treated my brothers and me like we were his kids. When he moved into our house, he used to take Kimani and me with him everywhere he went. Sometimes he'd race with us and our friends in the court. I remember he taught us how to fish. At first, I didn't even know what fishing was. I thought you just took a net and just got in the water to catch fish. I know that's crazy. He also taught us how to crab, which actually includes a net. We tied pieces of string to turkey wings and then tied the strings to a stick. We waited until we saw the string being pulled, grabbed the net, and scooped the crab from behind. Dewayne took them home and boiled them. He's a great cook. I like when he makes shrimp pasta.

The first fuss we had was about him putting me out of the car while his kids, Kimani, and our friends were still there. When he made it through the door later that day it was like World War III. I wanted to fight but just started crying. He left out the door and

Dewayne Clark, courtesy of Lynette Phillips.

I said, "You stupid bitch!" as loud as I could. I heard the next door neighbor call Dewayne and tell him what I said. He came back up the stairs and started banging on the door. I said, "You got a key, use it." He came in the door and asked me what I said.

I said, "Get out my face." He said, "Oh, faggot ass." And I said, "Fuck you. None of your children can fuck with me though. Send one of your children out here and watch what happens!" We moved past everything after I apologized to him. It wasn't my place to say all that. At the same time, it wasn't his place to say what he said. This happened like every year.

Despite our fights, I hope my mama and Dewayne get married one day. I say that because my mama says she's not going to ever get married and I think that she and Dewayne make a perfect couple. It seems like they're not going to ever break-up, so why not get married? She claims if they get married, she doesn't want a big wedding. I told her she doesn't have to have one, as long as I'm there.

KEEPS SAYING IT

Kenneth: Was I a troublemaker?

Lynette: No.

Kenneth: Do you think my daddy and I have similar personalities?

Lynette: No.

Kenneth: What makes you say that? That ain't funny, Ma.

Lynette: Why do you think? You answer it. Why do you think?

Kenneth: I really don't think we have the same personality, but everyone keeps saying that in the interviews.

Lynette: I know how you get—like the feedback, the talk back. Your daddy has got short patience—real short patience. I have been through so much. I can't explain. But I know you love your daddy.

Answer Your Phone

I thought I wanted to go into the Marines, but I changed my mind and my daddy got mad. We yelled at each other, sent nasty text messages, and then stopped speaking all together.

One day, I was sitting on the computer writing Kimani on MySpace. The name Florida popped up on my phone. I started not to answer but something told me, "All this has to end someday." I answered the phone. I heard a deep voice say, "What's up, son? You know who this is? This your daddy."

Me: Oh, what's up?

Dad: This beefing has got to end, dawg. Daddy's sorry. I didn't mean to say all those mean things to you. You are my son. I wouldn't do nothing to hurt you.

Me: Mmm…It wasn't my place to curse you out, man. I'm just going through too much right now. I could feel myself stressing.

Dad: You stressing? Shh, brah…Everything is going to be all right. Grandma told me you are writing a book, huh?

Me: [*Laughter*] Yeah, I am.

Dad: Yeah, man, daddy is proud of you. I really mean that. Dude, you're writing your own book!

Me: Thank you. It's better than just being on the streets.

Dad: You and your brother keep a smile on my face. You always were about your business when it came down to school.

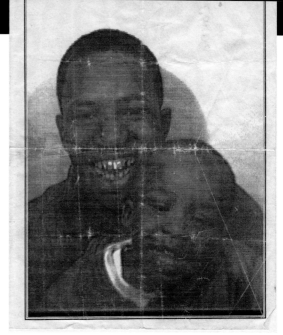

Kenneth and his dad, courtesy of Loretta Martin.

Me: Yeah I'm about to graduate next year. I'm getting ready to get up out of here. I'm ready to be on my own.

Dad: Daddy loves y'all. See, you and Kimani, y'all my babies—I love y'all to death. I want y'all to take that to y'all's grave or however it go. Kenneth, me and you, we're like that same person. We look the same, dude! You have my exact face. I couldn't deny you or your brother if I tried. Whatever you decide to do with your life, I'ma still love you. You're my very first son. I was 17 when your mama had you.

We're the triple K. We're supposed to stick together, not go against each other. You and your brother are tighter than any other brothers that I know. Y'all twins. Beyond that, y'all boys are best friends. I want to have that same relationship with you. I'ma call you when I leave out of this packed-ass grocery store.

Me: All right.

Dad: Answer your phone.

From left: Kenneth, Kimani, and Terrance, by Lindsey Darnell.

PEOPLE YOU CAN DEPEND ON

Kenneth: What makes you happy?

Lynette: Being on this Earth, surviving. I'm happy every day if I know that my kids and my family are okay.

Kenneth: What sorts of things do you like to do?

Lynette: Most of the time, I just watch T.V. Sometimes when I'm off from work, I wish I went to work because normally, just about every day I be at work.

Kenneth: If you had one wish, what would it be?

Lynette: Buy me a house. I wish I had a house. Buy me a nice car. Buy my kids cars to get around in.

Kenneth: Who was the most important person in your life?

Lynette: God. He's the reason I'm still here. My kids, my mom, family, people that you can depend upon.

NSP AFTERWORD

December 2009

It has been a long four years for the Neighborhood Story Project since the last series of books by John McDonogh students came out. In June of 2005, we were riding high, with five books by high school students circulating the city and neighborhoods were they were written. After Harry Potter, they were the best sellers in the city.

And in August of 2005 we were back at John McDonogh, with 60 applicants for the next round of book-making, and went home for a weekend of sorting applications. On Monday, the levees failed, and the applications were waiting on Rachel's kitchen table when we got back to town seven weeks later, a grim reminder of one more thing lost.

The NSP set about the work it knew, making books with Nine Times Social and Pleasure Club, making posters about the Seventh Ward, and a book of community gathering spots- Cornerstones. But through it all we wanted to go back to John McDonogh and hear what was happening in teenage-land.

So in the fall of 2007, we went recruiting at John Mac. We were holding the first round of books, relics of the pre-storm era, and very few of the new students had heard of them. There were five brave souls who signed up for a class in book-making. Daron Crawford, Susan Henry, Kareem Kennedy, Kenneth Phillips, and Pernell Russell.

The first part was the easiest. We read the first round of NSP books and the classics like: *Life and Death on the South Side of Chicago*, and Sherman Alexie's *Lone Ranger and Tonto First Fight in Heaven*.

And then we started on the two and a half year journey of writing our stories. We wrote about life before Katrina, and some of the Katrina experience, but we mostly worked on Documenting the Now.

The Now was ever-changing: Daron moved from house to house, and studio to studio. Kareem went from high school student to Delgado student. Pernell went from nearly care-free (dancing, making clothes) to dealing with loss. Susan's career in fashion and cosmetology went from theoretical to real. Kenneth worked on his anger management, while getting learning about his past.

We began to talk about the need to have something at stake in the book- the need to represent our struggles and not just the things that we wanted people to know about our lives. Or as Kareem Kennedy put it to everyone, "People want to read your mind to ease their mind."

And so we started in on the writing the hard parts. We went to where the projects were in the process of being torn down. Sneaking in through holes in fences, we roamed where the thousands lived, now desolate and post-apocalyptic. We went to the new spaces, shotgun doubles, ranch homes in the suburbs, and we wrote to make sense of the changes.

Rachel taught interviewing and ethnography- how to de-familiarize yourself with your surroundings and connect your personal stories to the larger cultures of New Orleans. Abram taught writing styles. Lea and Lindsey went with the writers to interview and photograph.

During 2008 we kept at it, interviewing family, former neighbors, other people who could help broaden their perspectives on themes in the books.

In March of 2008 the NSP published *The House of Dance and Feathers: A Museum by Ronald Lewis*, and the writers got to see their first NSP book release party- in Ronald's backyard in the Lower Ninth Ward, Mardi Gras Indians and Brass Bands. Two hundred people dancing in the rain.

As Rachel turned her attention from editing *The House of Dance and Feathers*, toward working on building up the structures of the four books the work kicked into overdrive. Weekends became an abstract idea, as writers and NSP staff started to live in our office in Seventh Ward. We took occasional breaks to go back out and get more photos, or to get the interviewees more involved in the editing process.

In September of 2009 we printed out what we had and gave copies to family and friends and impartial readers. They came together as book committees, telling us what they liked and what the books needed to feel finished. We took notes, gave ourselves a weekend off, and then got back on the horse.

October was the end of the road. We had to weigh what pieces stayed in, how to tell the untold parts. Hard decisions as the idea of books met the reality of paper and print. Late nights and early mornings led to this- four new books, five new authors, and a return to the roots of the NSP.

NSP'S HUGE LIST OF THANK-YOUS

Our first and biggest thank-you to our authors and their families: Daron Crawford, Susan Henry, Kareem Kennedy, Kenneth Phillips, and Pernell Russell. It has been two great years of getting to know y'all, and a huge honor to be so involved in your lives. We are proud of your work, and feel blessed to have become family. We look forward to knowing y'all and reading y'all for years to come.

To the mighty University of New Orleans—the College of Liberal Arts, the College of Education, and UNO Press: We are grateful and proud to be a part of the University community. Thank you to Chancellor Ryan, Susan Krantz, Rick Barton, Bob Cashner, Joe King, and Anthony Cipolone. In Anthropology, thank you to David Beriss, Jeffrey Ehrenreich, and Martha Ward. In the College of Education, thank you to Jim Meza, Andre Perry, and April Whatley Bedford. At UNO Press, Bill Lavender and GK Darby.

To all the people who have supported the NSP, thank you. Huge gratitude to all of the writers at the write-a-thon, without whom we could not have made this milestone. We look forward to out-writing last year's amazingness.

To the Lupin Foundation. Thank you for your consistent support over the years. These books could not have happened without you.

To our John McDonogh Senior High/ RSD family—Principal Gerald Debose, Antoinette Pratcher, Dawn Greay, Alicia Carter Watts, Shawon Bernard, Brother Jamal Robertson, Deborah Richardson, Nira Cooper and all of the other teachers at the Mac. Thank you for working with us and for being so supportive of the efforts of the NSP.

Thank you to the Cowan Family and Jewish Funds for Justice. Your gift kept us going, and Paul's legacy continues to inspire us.

To Gareth, thank you for going above and beyond, once again, to balance a crazy amount of work with beautiful design.

For getting us ready to go to press, Felicia McCarren, Jordan Flaherty, Siobhan Flahive McKieran, Ariella Cohen, GK Darby, Bill Lavender, Hot Iron Press, and Eve Abrams.

To the Bard Early College in New Orleans program and Stephen Tremaine: thank you for being an awesome partner in this work.

To our board—Petrice Sams Abiodun, Susan Krantz. Corlita Mahr Spreen, Troy Materre, Helen Regis, and Emelda Wylie. It has been a great journey with y'all, and we are looking forward to more.

Thank you to the Zeitoun Foundation for supporting the work. Your unsolicited gift was a huge boost to our organization, and your story of reclaiming against great odds has been part of our inspiration.

And to our families: Dan and Max Omar Etheridge; Cynthia Breunlin, Doug Breunlin and Nanci Gordon, Megan Etheridge, and Kate, Tommaso, and Zoe Weichmann (for stepping in to help take care of Rachel's men while she was on editing lockdown); Nolan Marshall, Tessa Corthell, Shana Sassoon, Phyllis, Linda and Jerry, the Hsiangs, the Downings, the Darnells: thank you for being our family through this process. We could not have done it without you, and we are glad we didn't have to try.

Viva New Orleans

Rachel Breunlin, Lindsey Darnell, Lea Downing and Abram Himelstein

Neighborhood Story Project